UNIQUE EATS AND EATERIES

OF

THE PEOPLE AND STORIES BEHIND THE FOOD

PAULA JOHNSON

Paula Johnson

UNIQUE EATS AND EATERIES

OF

THE PEOPLE AND STORIES BEHIND THE FOOD

PAULA JOHNSON

DEDICATION

This book is dedicated to my friends and acquaintances
in the restaurant and hospitality industry.
It is a pleasure to see your smiling faces around town.

And to all their grandmas who taught them how to cook.

CONTENTS

ACKNOWLEDGMENTS

A special thank-you to my family for their love, support, and inspiration.

Also, thank you to my dear friends Margaret Manley, Trudy Monaco, Jenni Schaming, Flo Ullrich, Jodi Bowlin Eades, and Emily Langford for their continuous encouragement and for understanding when our dining-out time was put on hold for writing time.

Finally, thank you to my buddy Grady Regas for sharing his extensive knowledge of the restaurant business with me and the city of Knoxville, and to the late Bill Regas for building the foundation of Knoxville's restaurant industry.

INTRODUCTION

The idea for a book about unique eateries of Knoxville came about shortly before a unique, unprecedented event—a global pandemic. It became a very precarious time all over the country and the world as businesses were forced to close for an undetermined amount of time, sending the hospitality industry into a panic. In Knoxville, our meticulously restored downtown that we were all so proud of reverted to the ghost town it was years ago.

But Knoxville is filled with people who love to eat and who love local restaurants. I heard a guest exclaim once, "I've never seen a more eating and drinking town than this!" Our community strived to support their favorite local businesses and restaurants during the pandemic and quickly jumped into action, ordering takeout, buying gift cards, and providing food for employees who suddenly found themselves out of work. The words "carryout" and "curbside" almost instantly became a familiar part of our lexicon. Any restaurant lucky enough to have a drive-through window or an outdoor patio had an advantage. Selling groceries, cocktail kits, and mixes were new, innovative ideas for traditional sit-down restaurants.

After many months, as the air started to clear, we began to see signs of life about town again. Businesses began to reopen their doors to the public, slowly at first, with limited seating in restaurants and tables spaced out for social distancing. Paper disposable menus or laminated menus for easy wipe-down sanitizing were implemented as were scannable codes for menus. Owners began to unexpectedly share information with me on a topic never before discussed—amounts of weekly or monthly sales or numbers of guests coming in.

Remarkably, most Knoxville restaurants survived the pandemic, and new ones even opened and thrived. As restaurants returned to full capacity, many had trouble finding enough employees to run their businesses at their regular days and hours. Managers were asking if I knew of any cooks I could send their way.

So, what is happening in Knoxville's restaurant scene today? In a way, this book picks up where my last book, *Lost Restaurants of Knoxville*, left off—with our "new downtown" paired with long-standing iconic Knoxville landmarks.

In Knoxville, eating is a social event: it's entertainment, it can be a hobby, and even at times, an extreme sport. Knoxville is home to over 900 different eateries—restaurants, cafés, diners, food trucks. I've taken the time and opportunity to explore and experience most of them. Here is a collection of locally owned restaurants from neighborhoods all around town—each with a unique story, space, cuisine, or lineage. These businesses are run by our neighbors and friends. I'd like to gather them up and give them all a big collective hug. I hope this local restaurant guide will inspire you to have some fun and venture out to discover some restaurants listed here along with the many other great eats all around town.

Welcome to Knoxville. Enjoy!

—Paula

UNIQUE EATS AND EATERIES

OF

KNOXVILLE

BISTRO AT THE BIJOU

A local favorite since 1980

"You got pretty good at telling my story," Martha Boggs, owner of Bistro at the Bijou, teased me. The iconic Bistro was one of the most popular stops on my tour and might be the first destination you want to visit while eating your way through Knoxville. Housed in the fourth-oldest building in town, the space has always been used as an eating and drinking establishment since its construction in 1816. While this building wasn't home to Knoxville's first tavern, it was home to its fanciest. Through the years, multiple United States presidents visited and dined at the Bijou when it housed a tavern and hotel.

In 1980, preservationist Kristopher Kendrick opened a restaurant at the Bijou that he called, simply, the Bistro. Down the street, near the University of Tennessee, Martha Boggs was employed in restaurants working her way through college. Eventually Martha arrived at her destination at the Bistro, worked her way up to manager, and finally bought the downtown restaurant in 2009.

Martha began cooking for her family when she was a young girl in Ducktown, Tennessee. At the time, "farm-to-table" wasn't a fashionable term for a trendy style of cooking and eating; it was a way of life. Martha continues in that manner with her offering of rotating seasonal menus. In addition to buying from and supporting local farmers, Martha and her husband have a five-acre garden on their property, and he is a gardener. In the perfect restaurateur–gardener relationship, they can plan together what he will grow that can be used in the restaurant in the form of daily chalkboard specials.

A favorite of locals, the Bistro also became go-to dining for vegetarians when Martha began preparing vegetables without

Left: Saturday brunch at the Bistro

Center: Owner Martha Boggs

Top right: Beet hummus

Bottom right: Seasonal salad

meat, which is common in Southern cuisine, to give her guests more options. Any veggie dishes at the Bistro can easily have proteins such as grilled chicken or salmon added to them. Visit for a taste of East Tennessee through their crispy fried okra or their pimento cheese fritters, Martha's recipe featured in *Southern Living* magazine. Come back for brunch on Saturdays.

While many guests love to dine at the Bistro prior to shows at the Bijou or nearby Tennessee Theatre, the Bistro also hosts weekly live jazz in the restaurant. Visit their sister restaurant Dazzo's across the street for authentic Italian cuisine.

807 S Gay St., 865-544-0537
thebistroatthebijou.com

> **The Bistro at the Bijou has consistently been named by different outlets as one of the 15 best restaurants in Tennessee.**

BROADWAY MARKET

If you know, you go

It is always truly a joy to visit with Lauren and Don DeVore, owners of Broadway Market. We talk about all the new and old restaurants, we laugh, and I leave with a fantastic amount of delicious and high-quality food.

Lauren and Don do it different; they do it their way. Other businesses dream of setting up on Market Square and Gay Street; Lauren and Don set up on Hill Avenue and let people come to them. And people do. Some restaurants are trying to cut costs with food and carryout containers; Lauren and Don offer premium seafood, choice meats, and even the best-quality to-go containers. Other owners have a slew of employees; Lauren and Don do it themselves. "I like to work," Don says. "I'm going to do the work."

Their dynamic partnership all started one night when Don decided to go down to Ruby Tuesday on the Strip to "meet some girls." Little did he know he would meet The Girl. Don and Lauren both graduated from the University of Tennessee, Don with a degree in English, Lauren in graphic arts. Though Don did want to pursue a career with his English degree, life happened. They became involved in the food world and never looked back. Lauren designed their logos and graphics and helps Don with all aspects of their business.

Don's cooking style developed from experience and cooking for a high volume of guests. He has worked in more than 20 restaurants including many years at the very popular Litton's in Fountain City. Don and Lauren took a moment of freedom and traveled to Seattle by bus and lived in a tent until he became a chef at Sound View Café in Pike Place Market. Later in Charleston he became a chef at Planter's Inn. Back home in Knoxville, they opened the Painted Table and Sequoyah Hills Café & Market.

Top left: Broadway Market dining room

Bottom left: Owners Don and Lauren DeVore

Top right: Spaghetti and meatballs

Bottom right: Tuna poke bowl with spring rolls

When Don saw a space available on Broadway, he knew it was the perfect place and size for their new Broadway Market. There, they developed a loyal following and became known for takeout, which was very helpful during the pandemic.

Make a reservation to visit their bigger place, now on Hill Avenue, for approachable food at a good price. Seared tuna poke, grilled salmon, shrimp and grits, haddock, jambalaya with chicken and smoked sausage, po' boys, fresh salads, and Don's homemade soups with corn bread are favorites. Get acquainted with Lauren and Don!

900 E Hill Ave., #130, 865-247-7543
knoxvillebroadwaymarket.com

"We are the rules. We make 'em, we break 'em."
–Don DeVore

MATT ROBBS
BISCUITS & BREW

With a little help from my friends

"What's that building?" many guests on my tour will ask and gesture toward the south end of downtown. The imposing Georgian-style building has a historic-looking facade; it was built in 1991 for the headquarters of Whittle Communications. Chris Whittle's communications company at one time employed 900 people, had annual revenues of $75 million, and published 21 magazines including *Esquire*. Following financial difficulties in the mid-90s, Whittle's Knoxville headquarters was shut down and sold to the government to become the Howard H. Baker Jr. Federal Courthouse. It is also now home to a quaint shop serving up made-from-scratch biscuits and coffee.

Matt Robbins, originally from Texas, moved to Tennessee and enrolled at Roane State Community College to study music. Although he led music and worship in church, he found himself heading more toward the food and service industry. He managed a Domino's Pizza near Chattanooga and later worked his way up to assistant manager at Starbucks and helped open a Starbucks on Emory Road in Knoxville. It was while working with these large corporations that he learned great customer service skills. In 2012, Matt moved to downtown Knoxville and became manager at local coffee shop Remedy.

A friend Matt played music with, Nancy Wilson, noticed how capable he was at running a business and asked why he didn't have his own business. It was the first time Matt had given the idea any thought. Since he had been making biscuits at home for his daughter, a biscuit shop came to mind. He began by doing pop-

Top left: Owner Matt Robbins

Top center: Choose biscuit toppings of flavorful jams or pimento cheese

Top right: Sausage biscuit filled with sausage and egg

Bottom left: Fresh-baked biscuits

Bottom right: Iced coffee

ups around town and delivering biscuits in his van. He planned to open in the First Tennessee Building but ran into friend Pierce LaMacchia, owner of K Brew, who showed him the courthouse space. Nancy, marketing phenom, created his social media and a Kickstarter project, which was fully funded by Matt's collection of friends and biscuit fans. In 2018, he opened Matt Robbs Biscuits & Brew.

With the Build Your Own Biscuit menu, guests choose a biscuit then choose from an array of toppings, like chipotle cream cheese or strawberry jam. Pair it with Matt's cold brew, a latte, or a cappuccino. Matt opens at 8 a.m. and closes when he sells out, or by noon. Locals and travelers form lines out the door on Saturdays!

800 Market St., 865-804-0278
facebook.com/mattrobbsbiscuits

Matt loves serving biscuits and coffee but really loves building relationships. He notes, "When you're good to people, it comes back on you."

DOWNTOWN DELI

Helping the community, one person at a time

"You got fired from Taco Bell!" I exclaimed. It's just one of the funny stories David Grant tells me when I go by his Downtown Deli on Gay Street. Others include how one of his regular customers whom he always "talked about everything" with, including Arkansas football, one day came in with a team of football coaches from the University of Tennessee. When Dave wanted a picture of the Tennessee coaches but not "the Arkansas guy," the other coaches quickly let him know that he definitely wanted his guest in the picture because it was "like printing Tennessee money." Dave learned that he had been entertaining none other than Coach Johnny Majors. Then there's the one about the "scruffy-looking guy" sitting down next to him insisting he take one of his chicken wings—Market Square entrepreneur Scott West. Or the customer Dave thought was the weatherman from Channel 6, but was actually United States Representative Tim Burchett, who eventually got his regular order—the hot Italian sandwich—named after him.

Dave has a way with people. When he lived in Los Angeles in the 1980s, his neighbors were rock stars. As the band Great White was set to go on tour, their singer thought Dave was so fun to be around that he paid for him to go to bartending school so he could travel with the band.

Then, Dave decided to take this culinary stuff seriously. After receiving his training in Scottsdale, he took positions in five-star resorts, lodges, clubs, hotels, and inns around Arizona, Utah, California, and even Alaska. Working with accomplished chefs, his goal was to learn as much as he could. His accomplishments eventually accumulated to managing the hosting of Presidents

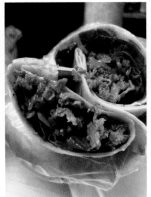

Left: Downtown Deli inside the First Horizon Bank building

Center left: Breakfast to go

Center right: Spinach wrap

Right: Dave's connection to the music industry

George H.W. Bush, Bill Clinton, and George W. Bush at the Arizona Biltmore in Phoenix.

The continuous ongoing events in the private dining arena can eventually cause stress and burnout for a chef. When Dave visited his son in Knoxville, he knew this was the place to open his own restaurant or food truck.

One of Dave's greatest achievements at the Downtown Deli might be helping others in the community. He has hosted cooking classes for kids, dropped off food left from the day for the homeless, and as a business owner who hires "second chance" employees, he works with the Helen Ross McNabb Center and the probation office to employ people who need a chance to get a fresh start in life.

800 S Gay St., 865-540-4141
downtowndeli-deli.business.site

Downtown Deli has provided the official postgame meals for Knoxville's Ice Bears for the past three years!

KoPita

Authentic Mediterranean

"We're coming to see you today!" I yell to Avi while he's taking a break on the patio of KoPita. "OK, what time?" he calls back. I remember the first time I ate at KoPita, I was having a pita stuffed with falafel, Arabic salad, sauerkraut, sumac onions, pickles, and tahini, and was trying to keep from spilling it everywhere, but Avi wanted me to take a bite with some of everything in it. He enjoys creating good food and likes seeing his guests enjoying their meals.

Avi Zenatti emigrated from Israel with his wife in 2007. He opened his vegan eatery KoPita in downtown Knoxville in 2019. Avi's knowledge of food preparation comes from cooking for his big family with recipes passed down through generations. Avi's father is from Morocco, and the food of KoPita is described as Mediterranean, Middle Eastern, and North African.

KoPita's dishes are healthy, beautifully presented, and delicious. The open kitchen allows guests to watch their food being freshly prepared. They have plenty of vegan options, like salads and falafel bowls or even a whole roasted cauliflower. Their pita is imported from Israel for meals like shawarma vegan pita and the sabich pita, which combines eggplant with tahini and harissa.

For a sampler of many things, order a mezze platter, which features hummus, babaganoush (fun to say, even more fun to eat), falafel, daily veggie salads, and pita. Accompany your meal with a complimentary hot cup of Moroccan mint tea. For dessert, baklava

> **Make a reservation to experience one of KoPita's monthly first Friday Shabbat dinners!**

Left: Variety of Mediterranean dishes
Middle: Falafel bowl with Arabic salad
Right: Vegetable salads from the mezze platter

is KoPita's sweet, nutty, vegan dessert drizzled in syrup, or end your meal with a Turkish coffee and bowl of mixed nuts.

Eventually, when the space next door to KoPita became available, Avi opened KoPita Meat. Options there include pitas, which can also be made into plates with larger portions, a variety of side salads, and roasted potatoes or rice. Pitas include the chicken and lamb shwarma, spicy merguez sausage, a classic kebab of lamb and beef, schnitzel fried chicken, and even chicken liver with preserved lemon. Groups of four or more can indulge in the Welcome to the Family tasting platter.

Finally, Avi decided to combine the meat and vegan restaurants together with the meat dishes prepared in the back kitchen while the veggies are still prepared in the open kitchen up front.

524 S Gay St., 865-249-8823
kopitarestaurants.com

FAI THAI KITCHEN

Authentic Thai Cuisine

"It's Paula, right?" Fai greeted me at her Gay Street shop, Fai Thai Kitchen. I was so surprised she remembered me after just popping in a few weeks earlier. Fai considers her intimate, family-run restaurant to be a home she welcomes guests into. Husband Nathan Blais helps out and Fai's mother, Suri "Tik" Wattanakul, and her dad, Chatchai "Fa" Puchakanit, do much of the cooking.

In 2018, Kultida "Fai" Blais opened her food truck—Fai Thai—cleverly using the Thai nickname her mother gave her, which means "cotton," for her fair skin. Originally from Bangkok, Thailand, Fai studied journalism and graduated with honors from Bangkok University. Fai's parents had moved to New York and in 2014 she decided to join them to study English. The family moved to Knoxville through her parents' work and Fai enrolled in the English Language Institute at the University of Tennessee. With a dream to open her own business, Fai obtained a loan from the Knoxville Area Urban League designated for minority-owned businesses.

During the pandemic, Fai and Nathan took a break from the food truck and Fai was able to stay at home with their newborn son. When a space became available on Gay Street in 2021, complete with restaurant equipment, Fai decided to go for it. The clientele she built with the truck followed her to the brick-and-mortar space and the business developed new fans at its prime location near the theaters and Krutch Park.

Many of the dishes at Fai Thai are "Grandma recipes" passed down from Fai's grandparents. In addition to honoring her grandmother in this way, Fai's goal is to provide quality, consistent food with a great taste. Fresh veggies are prepped daily for plates cooked to order. Fai's father became the head chef at an acclaimed

Top left: Owner Fai and her father

Top center: Gay Street skyline c. 1900. With the turn of the century, new businesses have moved in, and it is home to Fai Thai Kitchen as well as other great Knoxville staples. Courtesy Getty Images.

Top right: Basil stir fry and drunken noodles

Bottom left: Chicken and veggie gyoza

Bottom right: Mom's kanom jeeb

restaurant in New York at age 22. When pressed from the restaurant owner after tasting his food about how he learned his recipes and where he went to culinary school, Fa insisted he had learned everything from his mother. Bestsellers are gluten-free pad thai and curry, drunken noodles, and vegan basil stir fry.

Fai feels having her spot on Gay Street is beyond what she dreamed of when coming to the United States. With her bright mind for business, willingness to take risks, and family by her side, the sky is the limit for Fai!

522 S Gay St., 865-474-9631
faithaikitchen.com

For dessert, try the tangy and refreshing mango sticky rice, a sweet Thai iced tea, or creamy Thai coffee.

NAMA SUSHI BAR

Your premier sushi bar plus new concepts

In 2003, an $8 million revitalization was completed on Knoxville's Market Square in an effort to revive and bring more business to the downtown area. Greg White was living and working downtown at the time and loved the sense of neighborhood in the city. As I've heard from other downtown business owners, Greg just wanted to be part of the redevelopment of the area. By 2004, he decided to open his own "cosmopolitan" restaurant on the 100 Block of Gay Street, Nama Sushi Bar.

Greg hoped that Nama would bring more life downtown. The small space with the sushi counter was immediately embraced and supported by downtown residents, workers, and explorers. Greg noted that his biggest fan was Harold Shersky, who had operated a Jewish delicatessen two doors down from Greg's new venture since 1948.

In 2006, Greg bought a building on Market Square for his second restaurant, La Costa, an "upscale casual" Latin eatery. A big focus of La Costa was being an environmentally conscious "green" restaurant—utilizing the recycling of paper products and cooking oil, nontoxic cleaners, and fluorescent lighting, as well as conserving water, using locally grown produce, and even serving organic wines. Another innovation of La Costa was offering locally brewed beer. Although that is the norm and expected now in restaurants, at the time, it was a new idea for Knoxville.

I viewed the inventive new restaurants La Costa and Nama as the beginning of our new downtown. While La Costa closed, the community connected with Nama. Greg went on to his true love of creating green businesses and sold the restaurant in 2009. The company has now grown from that one sushi counter to three full-scale restaurants in Knoxville and two in Nashville.

Left: Avocado and tomato salad
Right: Hot Nama: Asian fusion veggie and steak bowl

Nama LLC opened Harvest Land, Sea, & Vine in the Bearden District in 2019. Harvest features a rotating menu based on the changing seasons and incorporates products from local farmers. Koyo opened in 2021 as Nama's newest addition downtown on Clinch Avenue. It showcases elevated Japanese dining in two ways—*kore ni shi-masu*—"I'll choose this one" (order from the menu) and *omakase*—"I'll leave it up to you." Koyo's omakase sample is a four-course chef's feature at market price. Koyo has received accolades and the young restaurant already has a claim to fame—legendary musician Elton John ordered from Koyo while in town for his latest concert.

506 S Gay St., 865-633-8539
namasushibar.com

Nama features select half-price sushi rolls every Monday and Thursday, a great way to try something new!

CRUZE FARM ICE CREAM

Work hard, love harder

"Well, you know Colleen, she's a master marketer," a foodie friend remarked to me. I would agree, and also add that Colleen Cruze Bhatti is a master planner. I'd see Colleen around town, writing in a notebook, probably planning her future ice cream empire. She is definitely a great marketer, planner, and role model for girls and guys who want to create their own business.

"How ya gonna keep 'em down on the farm after they've seen Paree?" Judy Garland sang. For Colleen, it seemed an easy decision to return to the farm and help her family grow their milk business. Her parents, Cheri and Earl, sold pasteurized buttermilk and whole milk from their dairy farm at the farmer's market and to local individual customers. After Colleen graduated from the University of Tennessee, she began setting up wholesale accounts with Knoxville restaurants. Chefs around the country now praise Cruze Farm Milk.

The family bought a food truck to sell ice cream out of and added a stove to be able to offer more food sales such as biscuits, hot dogs, or burgers. Testing the market, in 2016, Colleen and husband Manjit opened a temporary warm-weather retail shop downtown on Union Avenue to sell ice cream and milk. The following year, they opened another temporary shop on Gay Street and opened a shop at the Asbury House, in the community where Colleen's grandparents had a dairy farm. In 2018, they added the Pizza Barn at Asbury.

> **Cruze Farm opened their third location at the Five Oaks Development next to the Ogle Brothers General Store in Sevierville at 1642 Parkway!**

Left: Butterscotch shake

Center: Permanent space in the Miller's Building on Gay Street

Right: Bright dining room with a retro look

Feeling comfortable enough to set up a year-round, permanent location in downtown Knoxville, Colleen and Manjit took a space in the Miller's Building on Gay Street later in 2018. Their shops are full of their "farm girl" staff in their instantly recognizable uniforms of red gingham dresses and bright red lipstick. They also now offer light milk, coffee milk, chocolate milk, and seasonal flavored milks at the shops as well as stores around town. The ice cream is all now soft serve and of course part of the fun is discovering flavors of the day.

445 S Gay St., Ste. 103, 865-333-1265
cruzefarm.com

PHŒNIX PHARMACY AND FOUNTAIN

Downtown pharmacy with classic soda fountain

The Phoenix Building was the first to be rebuilt after the "Million Dollar Fire" of Gay Street in 1897. It rose from the ashes in 1899 as a wholesaling warehouse and was Fowler Brothers Furniture for over 50 years. In 2015, it became home to the Phoenix Pharmacy and Fountain. A survey to downtown residents asked what it would require for Knoxville's downtown to be fully functional; a pharmacy was mentioned most often.

Local pharmacist Ron Sherrill was a pioneer of home health and long-term care. He operated his own company for around 40 years providing pharmaceutical care and medication delivery. Ron felt that the downtown needed and was ready for more service-oriented businesses, and he had been looking for a space to establish a downtown pharmacy. A pharmacy would make the area more sustainable, walkable, and would help Knoxville make the transition to a fully livable downtown. He also wanted the pharmacy to be in conjunction with an old-fashioned soda fountain, a gathering place that would build a sense of community.

Ron's son, Nolan Sherrill, was involved with bringing the project to life, as well as Ron's friends Bud Albers and Bud Kelly who brought a wealth of knowledge about Knoxville's history and pharmacy memorabilia. Local antique dealer Dale Honeycutt helped Nolan fashion the shop in the style he envisioned with restored furniture treasures. It was Nolan who would run the fountain.

Nolan's first career began in 2002, in Washington, DC, working in international security. Although his degree is in business administration, his work with the government managing big projects

Left: Ice cream and accompaniments are made in-house for amazing sundaes

Right: Old-fashioned focus on excellent service

with big budgets, being goal oriented and flexible, and interacting with high-level military officials and even the president of the United States are experiences that helped him attain success in business. He took a graduate-level ice cream–making course and also studied with Ray George of Tic Toc in Loudon. When Nolan's equipment arrived, Ray came to the Phoenix and worked with him in the new commercial kitchen in the basement of the building.

Nolan has a natural affinity for cooking and likes to do everything "the hard way," by scratch, and with genuine authenticity. Some of his recipes have been passed down from his great-grandparents. Sometimes he creates dishes and flavors based on memories. For Nolan, his new career is all about being at home in Knoxville, being around family and friends, and making a lasting impression.

418 S Gay St., 865-692-1603
thephoenixknoxville.com

Nolan said that I could tell people about his work with our national security or about his spot on the television show *Food Paradise*. But he says what he is most concerned with is being known as someone who wants to make great things and do what he can to help a few others along the way. Try his menu of specialty sundaes, small-batch ice cream, hand-spun shakes, floats, and hand-mixed drinks and sodas soon!

MAPLE HALL

Eat, drink, bowl

"We heard there is an underground Knoxville." There is! Along the 100 Block of Gay Street you can look down and see the original street level. When the train station and depot were built, there was a very steep hill to get up into town, so the viaducts were added to raise the street level. There were already businesses on the block, which became really nice basements, and the building continued on the new level. Most of that space is now blocked off or has been renovated into office space. But, if you want to have an underground experience in Knoxville, head to Maple Hall on the 400 Block.

Maple Hall is an upscale, underground bowling alley and lounge that showcases a full food menu along with craft cocktails and mocktails. The building was home to the downtown J. C. Penney store until it closed in 1980. The structure sat completely empty until 2013, when Maple Hall took the basement and back space while another new business in town, Babalu, took the adjacent side. Downstairs at Maple Hall, partake in one of the 11 bowling lanes, or unwind in a nook on one of the comfy leather couches and enjoy some made-from-scratch menu items filled with local ingredients.

Upstairs and around back, discover the hidden gem, the Maple Room, only accessible from the promenade. The modern space features extra-large, "life-size" board games, presents weekly trivia

> The Babalu remodel includes beautiful booths or "pods" that can be reserved for specialty tasting experiences such as extra-large charcuterie boards, family-style paella, or dessert flights.

Left: A Tennessee stack
Top center: Maple Hall mocktail
Bottom center: Seasonal salad and kombucha
Right: Back patio on the promenade

and music bingo nights, and is a regular host for Knoxville History Project programs as well as others. At the Maple Room, guests can experience the same food menu as Maple Hall, but they also get a specialty cocktail menu not available downstairs.

Some menu highlights include their bacon jam burger or their Tennessee stacks, which offer different meat and cheese options over fries, potato tots, or chips.

During the pandemic, Maple Hall's next-door neighbor Babalu decided to close permanently. After pondering the idea, the owners acquired and reopened the Knoxville Babalu in a bohemian, eclectic style.

414 S Gay St., 865-249-8454
maplehallknox.com

SUTTREE'S HIGH GRAVITY TAVERN

Beer, ramen, and games

I always say Knoxville is a major Southern city but at the same time, a small town. Some might even say one degree of separation. Before I began my tour, I used to eat brunch every Sunday at the Sunspot, a quirky and progressive eatery near the University of Tennessee. That's where I met Anne Ford and Matt Pacetti. After several years of experience working in the hospitality industry, the husband-and-wife team opened their own unique spot on redeveloping Gay Street in 2012.

From their travels, Anne and Matt had visited bars serving high-gravity beer and retro arcades in other cities. Their idea was to combine the two. While a new business venture is always a risk, the duo felt confident enough that their concept would be successful to try it.

Those new to town may not yet recognize the name Suttree. Mr. Suttree is the main character in the semi-autobiographical novel by one of Matt's favorite authors, Pulitzer Prize winner Cormac McCarthy. The story takes place in Knoxville in the 1950s where Cornelius Suttree descends from a well-to-do family but wants to give it all up to live on a boat on the river.

Suttree's features 32 constantly rotating taps of unexpected and unusual beer, some brewed locally in Knoxville, and others from all around the country. They also carry top-shelf bourbons and a liquor selection that rotates monthly. A knowledgeable staff is available to assist with your selections.

Food at Suttree's began as sandwiches and items sourced from local restaurants in a limited six-by-six-foot kitchen. It soon became apparent to Matt and Anne that a bigger preparation area would be needed to expand their food business to support their customer base.

Top left: Harrogate's Lounge retro arcade

Top center: Pepe's quesadilla

Top right: Gay Street location

Bottom: Royal with cheese

The kitchen and menu evolved, and their very popular ramen wasn't exactly planned but came about as more of an accident derived from Matt's affinity for Asian food. It is now 90 percent of their food business. The key to the flavorful ramen at Suttree's is fresh local ingredients. The smoked pulled pork and beef brisket are provided by Oakwood BBQ while the kimchi is made by the ladies at the Oriental Market on Sutherland Avenue.

The other side of the building contains Harrogate's Lounge (Harrogate is another McCarthy character), the retro arcade where Matt and Anne have created a fun environment for a mix of clientele of all ages.

409 S Gay St., 865-934-3814
suttreeshighgravitytavern.com

Visit Harrogate's Lounge to view a one-of-a-kind light-up pinball bar and play vintage games such as Galaga, Skee-Ball, foosball, NBA Jam, and a variety of pinball.

STOCK & BARREL

Gourmet burgers and bourbon

Stock & Barrel opened on Market Square in 2013 in a modest-sized space with a menu packed with big, bold flavors. It became an instant Knoxville classic. The focus of Stock & Barrel is, of course, gourmet-style burgers and rare and high-end bourbons. The goal is to obtain ingredients from farms within the area to promote local economic sustainability within the community. All-natural, pasture-fed, hormone-free beef is sourced from Mitchell Family Farms in Blaine, Tennessee. Burger buns, dusted with a specialty flour, are supplied by Flour Head Bakery.

Stock & Barrel was created by brothers Bill and Niko Angelos who had previously worked at their family's restaurants in Morristown and Angelos' at the Point on Douglas Lake in nearby Dandridge, a steak and seafood restaurant. Their new eatery was awarded Knoxville's Best Burger during its first year of business. Although Stock & Barrel offers over a dozen different varieties of burgers including a bison burger and a greek lamb burger, the bestseller is the classic bacon burger. Add some of their decadent duck fat fries and save room if possible for a luscious Nutella shake.

In 2016, Ben and Niko, along with friend Ben Austin, branched out with their new rustic and industrial-style eatery, Chivo Taqueria at 314 South Gay Street. While Stock & Barrel focused on burgers and bourbon, Chivo centers on tacos and tequila, featuring the largest selection of tequila in the Eastern United States. The name "Chivo" means goat, which appealed to the Angeloses whose grandparents had been goat herders in Greece. Local favorite Chivo uses non-GMO white dent corn from the area combined with other heirloom-variety corn from a Mexican cooperative for their house-made tortillas. The corn is soaked in

Left: Beer-battered onion rings
Center: Stock & Barrel dining room and bar
Right: Duck fat fries

lime before being ground on-site into masa. Nachos, quesadillas, and burritos are also popular here.

Bill, Niko, and Ben formed another new restaurant concept in 2022 with their seafood and oyster bar, the Brass Pearl, at 24 Market Square. The trio's love of oysters took them to visit a variety of raw bars around the world. Back home, they planned and created Knoxville's only raw bar. The Brass Pearl offers a rotating variety of East and West Coast oysters along with seasonal and sustainably caught seafood brought in daily. Make it your next evening out for a rich lobster bisque, flavorful fisherman's stew, luxurious seafood tower, or decadent osetra caviar.

35 Market Square, 865-766-2075
thestockandbarrel.com

Visit Stock & Barrel and Chivo for lunch or dinner. If you decide to head to the Brass Pearl, be sure to make reservations for dinner from 4 to 10 p.m. daily.

NOT WATSON'S KITCHEN + BAR

Making memories

In 2009 the "soccer senoritas" Viviana Nicholas, Nelia Kirtley, Marilyn Parham, and Stefanie Houser brought a second location of Soccer Taco to Market Square after having operated in the Bearden District since 2005. With its large selection of authentic cuisine, the Mexican-style restaurant and sports bar has always been a favorite of all my friends. Look for unique dishes such as pozole and lengua or cachete tacos along with traditional burritos, enchiladas, fajitas, tamales, and tortas. In 2016, a third Soccer Taco opened in the Northshore Town Center.

Meanwhile, on Market Square, a space became available near Soccer Taco, which had been the Watson's department store—the last big department store to leave the downtown area in 1992. Glen Kirtley remembered a fun story about Watson's. When he was a kid, his mother loved Watson's and spent hours shopping there. Many Saturdays the family would load into the car and the question would be presented, "Where are we headed?" The kids, uninterested in an afternoon full of shopping, would answer, "Not Watson's!" Fast-forward to 2014, when the team and Glen, Ron Houser, and Marilyn Parham opened Not Watson's Kitchen

In 2020, the team also took ownership of Myrtle's Chicken and Beer, a concept that had opened right next to Not Watson's on the Square but had closed during the pandemic.

Left: Veggie power wrap with fresh fruit

Center: Fried green tomatoes and pan-seared scallops

Right: Located at the former Watson's department store on Market Square

+ Bar. Not Watson's adds a vibrant spot to Market Square and a commitment to using the best ingredients sourced from local farmers.

For lunch and dinner, start with regional favorites like fried green tomatoes with pimento cheese, country ham, and tomato jam or pork belly tacos with cucumber slaw. My choice is the pan-seared scallops, but the tuna poke is great too. "Greenery" includes a large selection of salads including a flatiron kale caesar and warm bacon and spinach with grilled salmon.

They even have a great brunch menu with everything from chicken and biscuits to bacon omelets to French toast with their bourbon maple syrup.

15 Market Square, 865-766-4848
notwatsons.com

OLIVER ROYALE

Innovative and seasonal new American menu

There's a well-viewed comedy skit called "Is it classy enough?" Located in the anchor Peter Kern Building at the corner of Market Square is probably the classiest restaurant in Knoxville: the Oliver Royale. Here, you will experience a home of exemplary service and thoughtful food.

Civil War soldier-turned-baker, Peter Kern was so successful in his wholesale bread baking business that he was able to have his impressive Italianate, three-story building constructed on Market Square in 1875. Many years later, the upper floors were remodeled into a hotel for the 1982 World's Fair. Local preservationist Kristopher Kendrick bought and saved the property, along with many others in downtown Knoxville, and took up residence there. Regular guests of Kendrick's, now dubbed St. Oliver Hotel, inclued actress Patricia Neal, and it was here where author Elizabeth Gilbert finished her bestselling book *Eat, Pray, Love*.

Following Kristopher Kendrick's passing, Ethan Orley and Philip Welker purchased the historic building and opened their boutique Oliver Hotel in 2011. Their restaurant, the Oliver Royale, followed shortly thereafter in 2015. HoMe Design of Brooklyn was enlisted to create the modern design of the restaurant space with bold metallics and basket weave tile along with the uncovered original wood flooring of the building. The menu would be dubbed "New American."

The Oliver Royal features a seasonal menu with a focus on regional products and works with local, organic, and sustainable sources whenever possible. Purveyors have included Mountain Meadows Farms, Flour Head Bakery, and Springer Mountain Farms.

Left: Table setting for large party

Center left: Sunday brunch

Center right: Peter Kern Building, before it became home to the Oliver Royale. Courtesy of the Knoxville History Project.

Right: Fanciful dessert

Brunch is served Friday, Saturday, and Sunday mornings until 3 p.m. Fresh-baked biscuits and pastries, cornflake-crusted fried chicken with stone-ground grits, steak and eggs, a brunch burger and a variety of Benedicts are featured items. Choose a brunch cocktail or the Royal Refresher—the bartender's choice mocktail.

Dinner is served every day beginning at 4 p.m. Start with a baby lettuce or heirloom carrot salad, mussels, pork belly, or an artisan cheese and charcuterie board. Entrees may include confit short rib, pork chops, steaks, duck, house-made pastas, and a variety of fish dishes, but meals change with what is seasonally available.

At the Oliver Royale, they try to make available a vegetarian option in each course and can also accommodate food allergies and other dietary restrictions. This small and stylish restaurant can seat up to 65. A tight-knit staff works closely together to provide a personal experience for guests. Become a regular and you will be greeted upon arrival by name. Definitely classy.

5 Market Square, 865-622-6434
oliverroyale.com

After dinner, slip out back to the Oliver Hotel's Peter Kern Library speakeasy.

J. C. HOLDWAY

Elevated regional and seasonal cuisine

Many East Tennesseans' grandparents and relatives lived through the Depression and cooked and ate what they grew. Chef Joseph Lenn's family from Rogersville was no exception. He even remembers his Uncle Joe telling him about hog-killing days and making country ham. While times are very different now, Chef Joseph is keeping the tradition of regional cooking alive, complete with a wood-fire grill, in downtown Knoxville.

Joseph grew up in West Knoxville and after high school took a job at the locally owned Butler & Bailey Market. There, he discovered he enjoyed cooking after finding quality foods in the market to experiment with at home. He decided to attend culinary school at Johnson & Wales in Charleston. Joseph quickly built up an impressive résumé, beginning with an internship at luxury resort Blackberry Farm, then moving on to Peninsula Grill in Charleston, the Capitol Grill in Nashville, and finally back to Blackberry Farm where he remained for 10 years.

In 2013, Chef Joseph became the first Tennessee chef to receive the James Beard Award for Best Chef Southeast. By 2014, he was beginning to think about opening his own restaurant. He knew it was super risky but was confident at the same time, and knew he wanted to remain in East Tennessee because he loves the outdoors. Joseph found a space in the Daylight Building, which was formerly office space for the Tennessee Valley Authority, and named his restaurant after his Uncle Joe. I remember hearing that J. C. Holdway enjoyed eating out for every meal and thinking that was a man after my own heart.

Guests at J. C. Holdway can request to be seated at the chef's counter to watch and interact with Chef Joseph and his team in

Top left: Crispy potato cake
Bottom left: Blue cheesecake with lemon sherbet
Top center: Chef Joseph at work
Bottom center: Rhubarb soda
Right: Dining room and artwork

the open kitchen or relax in the stylish, airy, window-lined dining room. Throughout the restaurant is artwork by Amy Campbell, creator of the *Tennessee Farm Table* radio program, which highlights local food producers.

Chef Joseph describes his cooking style as "cooking within the seasons using regional ingredients to be inspired locally to make the familiar," and says it's important that it "tastes good." Specialties include house-made pastas and a prime ribeye.

501 Union Ave., 865-312-9050
jcholdway.com

Chef Joseph on creating a restaurant in his hometown: "I'm from Knoxville. I believe in this city; I'm going to do whatever it takes to make sure it works out."

PETE'S

Great food, great service, great value

"Did his dad really own Copper Kettle restaurant?" a guest on my tour recently exclaimed. "That was *the* place to eat!" Yes, Pete Natour's father and uncle ran the popular Copper Kettle and now Pete's two brothers each operate their own restaurants in Knoxville. Pete opened his restaurant downtown as Pete's Coffee Shop in 1986 and runs it with his wife, Rita, and son Joey. In recent years they began referring to the eatery as Pete's Restaurant to better represent the business, but their constant has been a goal to provide quality home-cooked food and they have built the business based on three Cs—courtesy, consistency, and cleanliness.

Pete and Rita's son Joey and his brothers grew up in the restaurant business just like Pete and his brothers and began helping out by washing cups at age eight. He became a cook and manager and attended the University of Tennessee as a business management major. While at UT, Joey won first place in a business plan competition by creating a smart restaurant technology system.

In 2002, businesses on the 400 block of Union Avenue had to vacate their spaces in the Sprankle Building, which had been purchased by Home Federal Bank with plans for their new headquarters. After being located at 428 Union Avenue for 16 years, Pete moved to his current location in a retail space in the new Locust Street Garage. The sleek new diner could accommodate 80 guests and included a lunch counter, which Pete's father insisted on because many patrons come to lunch on their own.

Everybody eats at Pete's—downtown workers, university students, local celebrities and athletes, and even new visitors to town who have been referred to the diner for a satisfying breakfast. Celebrity sightings have included actors Harrison Ford, Kiefer Sutherland, Lou Ferrigno, and Richard Grieco.

Left: Ultimate three-egg omelet

Right: Breakfast club with home fries

Pete and Rita's sons have their own namesake menu items—Cameron's club and Sami's club. Burgers are very popular for lunch as well as the homemade chicken and tuna salads and pimento cheese. Their daily specials with one meat option and two sides allow for unique meals every day of the week. Breakfast is served Monday through Friday from 6:30 a.m. until 11 p.m. with lunch until 2 p.m.

540 Union Ave., 865-523-2860

petescoffeeshop.com

Pete's team can come to you and provide catering or box lunches for your party, special event, or meeting. Or swing by and pick up some of their party trays to go! Pete's is also available to reserve after regular business hours for special events with customized menus.

YASSIN'S FALAFEL HOUSE

Nicest place in America

"Is he really that nice?" my friend asked. A smile came across my face at the reference—everyone knows Yassin's Falafel House in Knoxville, Tennessee, was voted "Nicest Place in America" in 2018. The contest was through *Reader's Digest*, partnered with *Good Morning America* and *USA Today*. Nominations were requested, and three individuals nominated Yassin's Falafel House restaurant. Yassin is noted for his welcoming demeanor and the inclusive atmosphere of his business. He has noted that his shop is a place where all people can come together and feel safe, and his motto is, "Welcome all sizes, all colors, all ages, all sexes, all cultures, all religions, all types, all beliefs, all people."

Yassin Terou was a Syrian refugee who came to the United States in 2011. He began his food business by selling his now-famous falafel at a local mosque. At the mosque, Yassin met a friend who wanted to help him open a food business downtown. He began by offering two dishes in a space at the corner of Walnut and Church Streets—falafel and hummus. He spent $200 to buy plastic tables and chairs and officially opened his first shop in 2014. A natural entrepreneur, Yassin had previously spent time in Spain where he ran a shop selling shawarma. He was confident about his food but just wanted to make people in Knoxville feel happy and comfortable.

Through word of mouth and social media, Yassin's business immediately took off. He rarely does advertising but instead relies on outreach to the city by participating in community events and, of course, his outgoing and friendly personality.

In 2017, Yassin was featured in a short film by the company Square, highlighting small businesses in America. In the film, Yassin noted that when he first arrived in America not knowing

Left: Dining room at Cedar Bluff location

Center left: House-made hummus

Center right: Fresh baklava

Right: Owner Yassin Terou

any English, he was scared of almost everything. Through his experience, Yassin learned that the American dream can be real. He thanks Knoxville for adopting him.

After the popularity and success of his first restaurant, Yassin was able to open a second eatery in 2018 in West Knoxville at Cedar Bluff, 159 North Peter Road, in the Town and Country Commons. He will soon open a shop in Maryville and has plans to take his concept and safe space to many cities and towns in Tennessee.

At Yassin's, tasty and healthy food is made daily from the freshest ingredients!

706 Walnut St., 865-219-1462
yassinsfalafelhouse.com

Yassin loves Knoxville and stresses that it is home. "Home is where you feel love and give and receive love," Yassin states. Oh, and yes, he's pretty nice too.

THE FRENCH MARKET CREPERIE

Authentic French crepes

After traveling to and living part time in Paris, Susan and Allen Tate wanted to bring parts of what they loved from France back to East Tennessee. In 2008 they opened their French Market Creperie in the otherwise deserted Farragut Hotel. The Farragut Hotel was built in 1919 and named for David Farragut, the first man to be named an admiral in the Navy who was also born in Knoxville. He was involved in the Civil War, fighting on the side of the Union. Farragut helped capture the city of New Orleans and also Mobile Bay, where he uttered his infamous statement, "Damn the torpedoes! Full speed ahead!" In the 1970s and '80s, the building was converted into an office building, then left standing empty until Susan and Allen brought a bit of light and life back to it with their creperie.

The Tates ordered equipment from France and taught themselves how to make crepes. They sourced traditional and buckwheat flour from France for the true authentic flavor they had experienced. By 2014, Susan and Allen had achieved success and accolades with the French Market and expanded to a second location in Farragut at

---

The French Market serves Europe's best-selling coffee, LavAzza, and creates espressos, cappuccinos, and lattes made with LavAzza's special blend Super Crema. Always check their chalkboard for seasonal teas and coffees.

Left: Busy breakfast service

Center: Beignets and sweet crepe

Right: Blueberry and lemon curd crepes and chocolate and strawberry crepes

161 Brooklawn. In 2017, the old Farragut Hotel was slated to be converted back into a hotel, and the Tates decided to move their downtown location to a space on Clinch Avenue. The larger space includes a mezzanine and more room for their many loyal guests.

Many people find the French Market for its breakfast crepes and fresh omelets, but the large menu also features savory crepes such as roast beef, smoked salmon, and ham and swiss. Sweet crepes include salted caramel, cherry cheesecake, and Bavarian cream, and the best-selling crepe at the French Market is Nutella.

If you come for lunch, you also have choices like chicken salad, French onion soup, and baked brie.

412 Clinch Ave., 865-540-4372
thefrenchmarketknoxville.com

THE TOMATO HEAD

Serving fresh food downtown since 1990

The Tomato Head restaurant might be called the OG of Market Square. It opened in 1990 when downtown Knoxville was relatively quiet, save for the daytime workers. I think of the dedication of owner Mahasti Vafaie, working the dinner shift at another restaurant at the same time that she was trying to establish a lunch business at her own restaurant. Times have changed with the redevelopment of Market Square. Now, Mahasti has a following of locals and visitors waiting to experience the Tomato Head.

Mahasti was born in Iran, but when she was a teenager, her parents sent her to live with her sister, who was studying at Middle Tennessee State University. Although Mahasti obtained her degree in mechanical engineering, it was on a vacation to New Orleans that she decided she wanted to open her own restaurant. Having cooked with her mother and grandmother, she already made her own sauces, breads, and hummus.

The Tomato Head prides itself on freshly prepared and house-made menu items and working with local meat and produce purveyors. While food is the focus, the eatery also advocates sustainability by way of recycling and conserving energy; supporting the community and nonprofits to help improve the lives of the less fortunate; providing support for downtown events; and celebrating Knoxville culture and the arts.

Her famous hummus is available with blue corn chips or as a vegetable and pita plate. They also have many varieties of salads, and a favorite is the Benton's bacon salad with fresh spinach, mushrooms, and warm poppy seed dressing.

Top left: Fresh seasonal salad

Center left: Chicken salad plate

Center right: The Tomato Head founder and chef, Mahasti Vafaie shortly after she opened the restaurant in 1990. Courtesy The Tomato Head.

Top right: Harold Shersky breakfast pizza

Right: Patio dining

They also have sandwiches, and their Kepner melt with baked tofu is a crowd-pleaser. Pizza is available by the slice at lunch or 9- or 14-inch at dinner, or you can try their house-made lamb sausage for something different.

For brunch, you can enjoy biscuits and gravy, huevos rancheros, breakfast bowls, egg sandwiches, or build your own Belgian waffle. Mahasti created the Harold Shersky breakfast pizza herself, which is topped with scrambled eggs, cheese, smoked salmon, capers, red onion, and crema in tribute to the man who ran a Jewish deli on the 100 Block of Gay Street.

12 Market Square, 865-637-4067
thetomatohead.com

Mahasti and partner Scott's Flour Head Bakery prepare all their own breads and desserts each morning, not only for Tomato Head but also for other restaurants and local stores. Her Tomato Head Hummus, with its "decidedly un-subtle" flavor, is available for purchase on their website and in retailers across the South.

EMILIA ITALIAN

Simple, seasonal, Italian

"We ate at Emilia last night, and I asked her where she wanted to go tonight for her birthday, and she said she wanted to go back to Emilia!" What a great recommendation for Emilia, Chef Matt Gallaher's Italian restaurant on Market Square. Matt got a taste for hospitality early on while helping in his mother's catering and restaurant businesses. Although he obtained a degree in chemical engineering from the University of Tennessee, his work with Knoxville chef Holly Hambright steered him back to the culinary world. Matt went on to cook at Blackberry Farm with chefs John Fleer and Joseph Lenn. He then took to the road, cooking for touring musical acts such as the Eagles, Kings of Leon, Wilco, Neil Young, Tim McGraw, and Keith Urban. In 2011, after much training and experience, Matt became the personal chef for Governor Bill Haslam. In 2013, he returned to Knoxville and opened Knox Mason featuring Appalachian and Foothills cuisine, followed by Emilia in 2016.

Emilia is named after Matt's grandmother, Emily Jackson, and sister, Emily Cowan. The elegant space is big enough for everything to be made from scratch. Build a beautiful meal from your first taste of antipasti dishes of baby artichoke fritters, smoky salmon tartare, or house-pulled burrata.

They also have contorni (sides) like roasted beets with pistachio butter and slow-cooked carrots. Definitely add warm Paysan focaccia to accompany your house-made pasta. At Emilia, they create pasta shapes as they like for different dishes, such as campanelle with mushrooms, cavatelli with seafood, fusilli with Benton's bacon and poached egg, or orecchiette with Bolognese sauce. Try hand-rolled gnocchi with house-cured pork jowl or Shelton Farm polenta with meatballs.

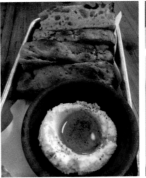

Left: Emilia on Market Square

Center left: Warm dining room

Center right: Paysan focaccia and Cruze Farm ricotta

Right: Pork Milanese

Mains include a Mitchell Farm steak, sustainable salmon, "under a brick" chicken, and pork Milanese. End your meal with a daily-spun sorbetto, tiramisu, or more.

Emilia is open for nightly dinner service beginning at 5:00 p.m. Tuesday through Sunday. Reservations are highly recommended for a taste of their take on house-made seasonal and regional Italian classics and local favorites.

16 Market Square, 865-313-2472
emiliaknox.com

Chef Matt's support of employee Blake Sallie's baking skills led them to becoming partners in Paysan Bread. Enjoy handcrafted Paysan bread with your meal!

PRESERVATION PUB

Keep Knoxville scruffy

"What is Scruffy City Hall?" many of my tour guests ask. It's one of Scott and Bernadette West's multilevel creative bar-and-restaurant concepts. Scott and Bernadette began with their original Earth to the Old City retail shop and expanded to multiple bars and restaurants on Market Square. Their mantra is: support local food, local music, local culture, local history, and local business. They have also kept Knoxville's "Scruffy City" nickname going strong.

The name comes from the 1982 World's Fair, hosted in Knoxville. As Knoxville was preparing for the fair, a reporter from the *New York Times* wrote an article and titled it, "What If You Threw a World's Fair and No One Came?" In the article, she made several disparaging remarks about Knoxville and called it a scruffy little city on the Tennessee River. Locals banded together to make sure the fair was a success and, after it was over, wore T-shirts and pins that said, "The Scruffy Little City Did It!"

Scott and Bernadette's Preservation Pub features live music 365 days of the year and four levels of fun, including the Moonshine Roof Garden. Guests can experience drink specials or build their own pizzas.

Right next door to Pres Pub is Scruffy City Hall, with its Gothic look and main hall for shows, a balcony bar, and a cinepub on the Scroof. Bernadette's Crystal Gardens at 26 Market Square features custom cocktails and 45,000 pounds of crystals over four floors—the Amethyst Lounge, Quartz Room, Rooftop Gemstone Garden, and Citrine Mezzanine. Private event space is available for rent in both Scruffy City Hall and Bernadette's. They both feature the same unique food menu as Preservation Pub.

Left: Preservation Pub and Scruffy City Hall on Market Square

Center: Rooftop bar

Right: The Scruffy City during the 1982 World's Fair. Courtesy Getty Images

Then there's Tommy Trent's Sports Saloon at 36 Market Square with its sports-themed dishes and quotes that line the large patio. The menu begins with soups, salads, and sandwiches. They also have pub fries in 6- or 12-ounce portions loaded with everything from beer cheese and chili to an all-beef patty, mushroom gravy, or pulled pork. A selection of wings, Scruffy dogs, and Tommy burgers round out the menu.

28 Market Square, 865-524-2224
scruffycity.com

Watch for the West's newest concept coming soon to Market Square, Alice in Appalachia.

BALTER BEERWORKS

More than a brewery

Balter Beerworks is a tale of two friendships. Blaine Wedekind and Will Rutemeyer were home brewers with a dream to open a brewery, but also a dream to be involved in the revitalization of downtown Knoxville. The building that became Balter was an old service station in a blighted area of downtown, at the corner of Jackson Avenue and Broadway. That section of Jackson is now filled with new businesses and residences, and a refurbished building right across Broadway became the home of the quirky and nationally renowned Glitterville Studio Store, filled with whimsical home and holiday decor.

One day, Blaine mentioned to his dad, David Wedekind, that he and Will were thinking of creating a brewpub after researching and discovering they really needed a food component in the business. David told them they should talk with his old law school buddy, Allen Corey, owner of Square One Holdings, a company that does exactly what Blaine and Will had in mind for downtown Knoxville: design and consult with restaurants and breweries to create unique made-from-scratch food and elevated bar programs.

Knowing they wanted to redefine and elevate the brewpub feel, but having no prior restaurant experience, Blaine and Will traveled to Chattanooga weekly to meet with members of Allen's

> Balter's efforts and hard work have had the desired results for their business and the downtown area. When it comes to neighborhood revitalization, Blaine's advice is, "If you want to build the community up, try to change it for the better."

Left: Dining room and bar
Center: Owner Blaine Wedekind
Right: Taco plate

team to work on menu development and attend food shows. The freshest ingredients including beef, breads, and produce from local purveyors Mitchell Farm, Flour Head Bakery, Sweetwater Valley Farm, Mahalo Coffee, 3 Bears Coffee, and others were incorporated into the Balter menu. Finally, by 2016, they opened their full-blown brewpub to the community, which inundated them with overwhelming support.

The lunch and dinner menus are refreshed often by offerings of seasonal and monthly specials. When you get there, start with an Appalachian favorite—fried green tomatoes with pimento cheese and tomato jelly—or try some blackened cod street tacos among other delicious options.

The brewpub's unexpected surprise was the success of brunch, accounting for 20 percent of Balter's business and now offered Saturday and Sunday 10 a.m. to 3 p.m. At their brunch, you can try anything from biscuits and gravy to breakfast quesadillas to chicken and waffles.

Also recommended for food and drink specials is Balter's happy hour, Monday through Friday from 3 to 5:30 p.m.

100 Broadway SW, 865-999-5015
balterbeerworks.com

A DOPO

Wood-fired sourdough pizza

It is fortunate when people know at a young age what they want to be when they grow up. Brian Strutz attended career day at his school dressed as a chef. He always wanted to own a restaurant and spent many years building up his skill set to be successful in his chosen career. At age 16, Brian began working at a restaurant with a wood-fired pizza oven and fell in love with the cooking style. He obtained a degree in marketing, worked as a television video editor, spent time working at Blackberry Farm, and worked in personal business and finance. He knew that to run a restaurant, he needed to have much knowledge about not only cooking, but also about marketing, accounting, staffing, problem-solving, hospitality, and customer service.

By 2016, Brian felt he was ready to open his own eatery that he called A Dopo, meaning, not goodbye, but only, "See you later." He reverted back to his experience with the wood-fired pizza to create Neapolitan-style pizza with a bubbly, charred sourdough crust. A Dopo was an instant hit, based on Brian's marketing background and ability to get a message out with his understanding of social media and positive responses to all requests for publicity, as well as the three major components of the restaurant—house-made sourdough, mozzarella, and gelato. The business was so busy that by 2018, Brian's wife, Jessica, left her teaching job and became an equal partner.

Make a dinner reservation to experience A Dopo's pizza rossa (red sauce) or pizza bianca (white sauce) with various toppings or add your own. For a special night out, ask for the "Trust Fall for 2" and let the chefs create your meal. Be sure and save room for small-batch gelato!

Top left: A Dopo on Williams Street
Bottom left: Kitchen and wood-fired pizza oven
Center: Sourdough focaccia with olive oil and red sauce
Right: Daily special pizza

Brian recently began leading the Knoxville Independent Restaurant Coalition, an organization to bring local restaurant owners together to communicate and discuss obstacles in their field and how to solve issues. The idea for the group was presented by restaurateur Randy Burleson, who specifically nominated Brian to be the lead.

Eventually, Brian and Jessica became interested in creating a new concept with colleagues Lawrence Faber and Emily Williams. The idea became reality in 2022 when the couples partnered to open Potchke, their cheeky take on the classic Jewish deli, in the Regas Building at 318 North Gay Street. Think blintzes, bialys, and babka.

516 Williams St., 865-321-1297
adopopizza.com

"Potchke" means to fuss about, dawdle, or waste time. I got a little laugh from Brian when I told him an Appalachian might call that piddling around.

OLIBEA

The creative life

Chef Jeffrey DeAlejandro comes from a creative family. His mother is designer Patricia Nash, whose luxurious leather handbags are sold in fine department stores around the country, and his father, Jeffrey Nash, is a developer who revitalizes and preserves historic buildings. It might surprise many to learn that Chef Jeffrey at one time worked on a construction crew, got his first degree in business, and had a dream of being a professional baseball player. To the delight of Knoxvillians, Jeffrey found his creative outlet in the culinary world.

Although Jeffrey is self-taught and learned from experience working with great chefs, he also completed the culinary program at the University of Tennessee. He began traveling the country to attend classes with master chefs and would work at their restaurants for free. He would also call and email in hopes of being able to meet and work with them. In this proactive way, he was able to meet most of the chefs he wanted to study with.

In 2007, while he was still studying at UT, Jeffrey and his parents opened the Crown & Goose, an English-style pub in the Old City, serving upper-end pub fare. When Jeffrey began changing up the menu every week and hosting special dinners, Knoxville, craving fine dining experiences, fell in love with what he was doing seemingly overnight. Chef Jeffrey was even able to get a loan to create his next dream, innovative breakfast and lunch spot OliBea, because the bank lenders were familiar with his food.

OliBea, named for Jeffrey's children Oliver and Beatrice, opened in 2014 at 109 South Central. The locally sourced breakfast and lunch menu allows Jeffrey to work with local farmers, offer new specials daily, and be at home to cook dinner with his wife and children. He notes that, "Being a good father is so important to me."

Top left: Blueberry pancake with cashews

Top center: OliBea breakfast plate

Top right: One of Chef Jeffrey's unique daily specials

Bottom: Dining room and kitchen

In 2020, Jeffrey moved OliBea to a bigger space just down the street at 211 South Central. The dining room offers seating for around 65 guests, nearly double the space of the original shop. The bigger kitchen presents opportunity for more recipe development. Best sellers are Chef Jeffrey's unique daily specials, the pickle-brined fried chicken biscuit, and the classic tacos. The OliBea Plate is guest's choice of style of eggs, potatoes, bread, and a side of smoked pork belly or sage sausage.

211 S Central St., 865-200-5450
olibeaoldcity.com

OliBea is often the first stop and introduction to Knoxville for guests of the tourism board, and visitors come into town specifically to eat at OliBea because of its features in *Food & Wine* magazine, the *New York Times*, *USA Today*, and *Southern Living*.

KAIZEN

Eclectic cuisine to expand your horizons

Although it is a bit off the beaten path, the space at 416 Clinch is a popular spot for food businesses and is always occupied. In 2016, Chef Jesse Newmister, a graduate of Sullivan University's culinary arts program in Louisville, Kentucky, opened Kaizen, his izakaya, a Japanese-style pub. Izakaya means "stay, drink, place"— it's a small space to relax and have drinks, snacks, and fun. Chef Jesse's izakaya is not strictly Japanese cuisine, but also incorporates other Asian influences including Szechuan and Thai.

At Kaizen, diners can begin with fried gyoza, crispy eggplant, pork egg rolls, or takoyaki—octopus fritters with pickled ginger. House specialties include chilled dan dan noodles along with other noodle dishes—Thai chicken, drunken lamb, and more. Steamed buns can be filled with anything from fried shrimp to tofu with hoisin sauce, but the best-selling dish at Kaizen is pork belly fried rice.

In 2018, Chef Jesse opened a second restaurant downtown, Tako Taco, at 235 West Depot Street, adjacent to the concert and event center Mill & Mine. Tako Taco features one of the best patios in town, where guests can relax with a view of the old Southern Railway Station. The cuisine is Latin inspired but uses Asian influences and techniques.

Delivery for Kaizen and Tako Taco is available through Loco–a cooperative delivery service owned and operated by local Knoxville restaurateurs who control the service through a board of directors.

Top left: Dumplings and noodle bowl

Top center: Tranquil dining room

Top right: Pork egg rolls

Bottom left: Kaizen courtyard

Bottom right: Steamed buns and best-selling pork belly fried rice

At Tako Taco, choose chorizo, chili-rubbed duck, or ribeye chicharron tacos on handmade corn tortillas made from masa that is sustainably sourced. Add a vegan and gluten-free guacamole, queso blanco, or salsa molcajete—a hand-ground salsa served with crispy tortillas. Empanadas, chicken taquitos, crispy pork ribs, and duck molletes are on the menu as well as nightly specials—Tuesdays, try the double decker taco, and Wednesday is Burrito Night.

In 2020, Kaizen moved to a different and bigger location in the Old City—a section of the building that had housed Crown & Goose. The large restaurant had been divided up into three smaller spaces, the other two taken by Hen Hoc Butcher and Deli and Honeymouth Leather, leaving Kaizen with the third space and, the piéce de résistance, the large outdoor courtyard. Make plans soon to visit two of the best outdoor dining spaces in the city and enjoy Chef Jesse's eclectic cuisine!

127 S Central St., 865-409-4444
knoxkaizen.com

SOUTHERN GRIT

Southern comfort food

"You know as much about this place as I do," B. G. DeHart jokes with me about his Southern and Low Country–inspired restaurant, because I have taken so many people there since he opened in 2019. Southern Grit is located on the ground level of a new development of luxury condominiums in Knoxville's Old City, the Crozier Building. John Crozier, along with other colleagues, established the award-winning East Tennessee Historical Society in the 1930s for the purpose of preserving documents of our original settlers. Central Street was formerly called Crozier Street, but the name was changed in the 1890s in order to standardize the city's addresses for the first time. This contemporary building with a name from the past is the perfect spot for B. G.'s new eatery to celebrate its Southern roots.

B. G. studied logistics and supply chain at the University of Tennessee and obtained a master's degree in operations from Belmont University in Nashville. Returning to his hometown of Morristown, he began working at a family-owned restaurant. After years of learning the business, he decided that if he was ever going to try to open his own restaurant, that was the time. The Southern Grit's stylish interior contains elements of both Knoxville and another of B. G.'s favorite cities, Charleston. He and his kitchen manager developed the menu with recipes based on the use of

> Visit Southern Grit Tuesday through Friday from 3:30 to 6:30 p.m. for happy hour, featuring pimento cheese and bacon fries, chargrilled wings, Buffalo chicken dip, and more.

Top left: Classic meatloaf, fried okra, mashed potatoes

Top center: Southern Cobb salad

Top right: Shrimp and grits

Bottom left: Happy hour fried chicken slider

Bottom right: Owner B.G. DeHart and guests

good, quality ingredients. A solid, reliable team helps run this busy establishment. Since the pandemic struck soon after Southern Grit opened, B. G. doesn't really know what a normal year is yet, but business is now steady.

Give B. G.'s restaurant a visit for Southern classics like shrimp and grits or their best seller, fried chicken. Brunch is also offered Saturday and Sunday 11 a.m. until 3 p.m. featuring biscuits with many varieties of toppings, and everything from fried biscuit donuts to hash brown casserole.

126 S Central St., 865-240-4275
thesoutherngrit.com

PAYSAN BREAD & BAGELS

Let them eat bread

Old North Knoxville is one of my favorite places to wander and explore. A turn off Central Street might take you past old industrial buildings, new art galleries, or even along historic cemeteries such as Knoxville National Cemetery, established during the Civil War by Union General Ambrose Burnside himself, or Old Gray Cemetery, the final resting place of many of Knoxville's early influential citizens. It's also an area where there seems to always be something creative popping up.

"Hello!" I call out to chef and baker Blake Sallie from across the street. He waits for me to catch up with him on the sidewalk, just around the corner from his shop on Tyson Street, where we enter an impromptu meeting next to the garbage cans. I find this amusing, but not completely unusual. Knoxville is an outdoor town, full of busy people on the go. I often catch up with colleagues in passing along the street.

Blake, originally from Bristol, is kind and earnest—everything you might expect a baker to be. After arriving in Knoxville, he took a job cooking at the award-winning Dancing Bear Lodge in Townsend. After the lodge burned down, he was offered a job by Chef Matt Gallaher at Gallaher's Knox Mason restaurant. It was at Knox Mason that Blake began experimenting with bread making. His sourdough-based bread making occurred organically. The first bread he made for Knox Mason was a "peasant bread" or country loaf. His focaccia bread was also perfectly suited for Matt's Italian restaurant, Emilia.

Aware that Blake wanted to start his own business, Matt joined him in his venture. They debuted Paysan Bread at the Market Square Farmer's Market in 2017. Paysan means "peasant" in French. By 2018, Matt had found a brick-and-mortar location

Top left: Handmade artisan bread at Paysan

Top center: Paysan owner Blake Sallie

Top right: Paysan bagels

Right: Paysan Bread at 804 Tyson Street

for Paysan—the former Maker's Donuts building on Tyson Street. Handmade sourdough breads, bagels, and spreads, along with a variety of seasonal toppings are offered at the shop. The small space is entirely a kitchen, but patrons can grab and go or even take their goodies next door to Remedy Coffee for inside seating. Blake created a website for online ordering, and you can still catch Paysan on Market Square at the Nourish Knoxville Farmer's Market. Stop by to pick up a baguette or what I called a "fancy French pastry"—a canelé, Blake reminded me.

804 Tyson St., 865-394-9840
paysanbread.com

Blake may have been surprised by the success and local demand for his "peasant bread," but you will feel like royalty savoring it.

FIN-TWO JAPANESE ALE HOUSE

Along the trade route

Many people think the term "Old City" refers to the oldest part of Knoxville. However, this area developed around the 1850s as the railroad was being built. Shops, eateries, and various other businesses popped up to welcome travelers and salesmen from the many passenger trains that came through Knoxville. Over 100 years later, preservationist Kristopher Kendrick began restoring and reviving buildings on Central. He mentioned his plans to a friend who replied, "Oh, Kris, that's the old city." Kendrick replied, "That's the perfect name for it!" From then on, "Old City" was used as a branding term for the area. Many of the buildings in the Old City are originals from the late 1800s, and now there is also new construction and a great new restaurant.

In 2019, Raymond Yip opened Fin-Two Japanese Ale House in the new Crozier Building. Fin-Two is in the izakaya style, and this sleek, simple, and modern space has become one of my favorite places to steal away to for a relaxing afternoon of many different small bites accompanied by a pot of hot tea and anime projected on the wall.

Some guests visit Fin-Two strictly for the ramen. The tonkotsu features a 24-hour bone broth, crispy pork belly, braised kale, confit

Visit Fin-Two for happy hour food and drink specials Monday through Thursday from 3 p.m. until 5 p.m. For large parties, order an omakase platter to dine in or to go and leave it to Raymond and his team!

Left: Happy hour nigiri selections
Center left: The Crozier Building on Central Street
Center right: Omakase sushi platter
Right: Sushi preparation in kitchen

shiitake, negi, nori, soft egg, and garlic oil. The tori shio is Springer Mountain bone broth with braised chicken, and yasai is a shiitake mushroom broth with kombu.

Yakitori are the small-bite skewers, priced right to try several or add with other elements of your meal. Try the short rib, a regional favorite, with shoyu glaze and wasabi or the kurobuta, a Japanese Berkshire sausage.

For sushi, Raymond uses up to eight different distributors to have the quantity of fresh product he needs to supply the restaurant. He created the Neighborhood Favorite Specialty Rolls as a fun nod to Knoxville. The Fourth and Eel and Godzilla in the Old City might give locals a giggle. Sundown features salmon and big-eye tuna, Appalachian Trail includes honeycrisp apple, and the Hall of Fame is a chef's specialty roll.

122 S Central St., 865-437-3105
fin-two.com

GOOD GOLLY TAMALE

Fast and delicious traditional comfort food

Knoxville has a surprising long history of tamales in its culinary landscape. Tamales were brought to town in the early 1900s by a fellow from East Tennessee who had run away with the circus (I'm not making this up). While working with the circus, he was put in charge of concessions. Through his travels, he became familiar with the tamale as a distinctive, hearty, and portable food and added it to his concession menu. Knoxville restaurants quickly caught on and began offering tamales as a specialty. Tamales are still red hot in Knoxville at Matt Miller's Good Golly Tamale.

The next spoken words from me or whoever I am talking with after one of us brings up Good Golly Tamale are, "It's sooo good!" That could have something to do with Matt's commitment to using "high-quality fat, and plenty of it." He utilizes Benton's bacon fat in the meat tamales and organic palm shortening in his veggie tamales.

Matt began his tamale adventure in 2013 at Nourish Knoxville's Market Square Farmer's Market, where he would transport his handmade fare on an industrial-type tricycle outfitted with a stainless-steel hot box. His tamale creations took off right away, and he would regularly sell out, prompting him to open a storefront location on Central Avenue in 2015. The shop sells out regularly too, and Matt is constantly working to replenish throughout the day, but you can give him a wave through the kitchen window.

The entire Good Golly Tamale kitchen is gluten free. Comfort food fast and nutritious is the order of the day. Matt uses organic, non-GMO corn masa, local produce, and locally sourced free-range meats. Daily tamale varieties include classic tamales as well as chicken tinga and queso poblano. The restaurant also has seasonal

Top left: Menu board

Top right: Tamale and sides

Bottom left: Black soup beans, curtido, collard greens

Bottom right: Bohemian dining room

and specialty tamales like chorizo with hot sauce, curry chicken, and the purple pig (tamales filled with purple sweet potatoes and pork cracklins). Flavorful sides are black soup beans, collard greens, Spanish rice, and curtido—fermented cabbage, onion, garlic, ginger, and spices.

112 S Central St., 865-337-5771
goodgollytamale.com

Vacuum-sealed frozen tamales in packs of two are available for purchase from the grab-and-go case at Good Golly Tamale. Simply heat and enjoy at your convenience!

BOYD'S JIG & REEL

Celebrating Scottish music, culture, and whisky

Some people think Knoxville's Old City—Jackson Avenue and Central Street, north of the massive Southern railyard—gained its name by being the oldest section of town. The oldest section of Knoxville is actually the other end of Gay Street, near the river. Old City was a branding term used by Knoxville preservationist Kristopher Kendrick as he redeveloped buildings in the area. Knoxville's Old City is anchored on one side by Patrick Sullivan's old saloon, and on the other by another historic building, now housing Boyd's Jig & Reel.

Following Randy and Jenny Boyd's extraordinary success with Randy's company Radio Systems Corporation, which sells over 400 pet-related products—including his breakout success, the Invisible Fence—employs over 700 people, and has nearly $500 million in annual sales in over 60 countries around the world, they devoted themselves to philanthropy. The Boyds support business, education, athletics, kids, pets, all things Tennessee, Knoxville, and the Old City, including a small musical pub with a very large whisky selection.

Jenny opened Boyd's Jig & Reel in 2011 with a mission of preserving and promoting the shared musical heritage of Scotland and Appalachia. Jig & Reel is a sessions pub, patterned after those in Edinburgh, where patrons can enjoy music, food, and whisky. Guests are encouraged to join in the fun of performing in music sessions by bringing their own instruments or choosing one from the wall. Sessions have included Scottish, Irish, strings only, bluegrass jam, Celtic jam for beginners and Scottish country dance. Live music is also held nightly featuring performers in genres of country, bluegrass, rockabilly, Americana, Cajun, indie-alternative, and singer-songwriter.

Boyd's Jig & Reel boasts a collection of over 950 varieties of whisky including Scotch, Irish, and Bourbon. With one of the largest

Left: Reclaimed windows from Regas restaurant and hanging instruments

Center left: Steak and ale potato jacket and fish po' boy

Center right: Sullivan's Saloon c. 1976 in Knoxville's Old City. The Old City is now home to restaurants like Boyd's Jig & Reel, which is across the street from this historic building. Courtesy Wikimedia Commons.

Right: Dining room and stage

Scotch whisky collections in the world, their goal is to represent every distillery including both those open and closed. Those who are new to whisky tasting might choose a flight or choose from the different regions of Scotland—Lowlands, Campbeltown, Islay, Island, Highlands, Speyside, or blended.

Want to pair your whisky with food? Jig & Reel features a menu of traditional Scottish and Irish selections including the house specialty fish-n-chips plus corned beef and cabbage, shepherd's pie, bangers and mash, haggis with neeps and tatties, Scotch eggs, smoked salmon, seafood chowder, and even sweets of sticky toffee pudding and fried Mars Bars.

101 S Central St., 865-247-7066
jigandreel.com

Stop by Boyd's Jig & Reel on Thursdays to try any of their Scotch whiskies by the half ounce at half off the regular menu price.

BARLEY'S TAPROOM & PIZZERIA

Live music, draft beer, pizza, and more

Barley's Taproom and Pizzeria on Jackson Avenue has a feeling of a business that has been there forever. But I do remember going to the Spaghetti Warehouse with friends in the late '80s and '90s in the same historic warehouse building the franchise restored in Knoxville's Old City. After the Civil War, Knoxville became known as a wholesaling center. The large railway brought in goods from all over and wholesaling warehouses were built along Jackson Avenue and Gay Street. Many of the buildings in Knoxville's Old City are original to that time period.

After Spaghetti Warehouse ran its course, the building was bought by business partners from Asheville to open another of their Barley's Taprooms. The Knoxville Barley's was sold to restaurateur Randy Burleson in 2002, who eventually sold it again to Thomas and Harrison Boyd in 2018.

Barley's is known for their large selection of beer with 96 varieties on tap and more available by the bottle, in addition to their well-stocked bar. They are also known for live music. View the upcoming nightly music and event schedule on their website and social media. Additionally, Barley's is now home to East Tennessee's own WDVX Blue Plate Special every Friday at noon. WDVX is a listener-supported, independent community public radio station with studios in Knoxville and Norris, Tennessee. The hour-long radio show is broadcast live and features two 30-minute sets by local or touring musicians and bands.

Left: Spinach con queso
Center: Brunch pizza and salad
Right: Large patio

The food menu features an extensive array of pizzas with sourdough crust and house-made herb tomato sauce in sizes of 12-, 14-, or 18-inch pies. Diners can also add up to 32 additional toppings and gourmet toppings to any pizza or build a slice during lunch. Other menu items—small bites, salad and bowls, burgers, sandwiches, and wraps—provide something for everyone.

Enjoy Saturday and Sunday brunch at Barley's from open until 2 p.m. The large covered porch is perfect for outdoor dining during the pandemic. Try a savory Rise and Shine Pie—eggs, bacon, smoked sausage, two cheeses, and aioli with alfalfa sprouts—or go sweet with the French Barley—cinnamon brown sugar crust, scrambled egg base, bacon, spinach, mozzarella, and maple syrup swirl.

200 E Jackson Ave., 865-521-0092
barleysknoxville.com

Rent Barley's Old Export Room or the Dewey Dining Room for private events and watch for new pairing dinners!

SCHULZES SCHNITZEL KITCHEN

At the castle

"And it looks like a castle!" Yeah, right, I thought, as someone excitedly described Schulz Bräu Brewing to me. Then one day as I was driving through Old North Knoxville, as I often do, it happened—I found it, on a side road just off Central. "I found the castle, I found the castle!" I excitedly thought to myself.

Nico Schulz created Schulz Bräu in 2016 to be a hub of authentic German culture, which would include a brewery, a food component, and space for traditional and special events. While Nico runs the brewery, his mother, Ilona, keeps the decor, food, and menus authentic. Nico's father, Wolfgang, helps with any maintenance needed on the brewing system, building add-ons, managing bar staff, and general guest enjoyment. Other family members are available to volunteer when needed, especially during busy times such as Oktoberfest.

Entering the adorable biergarten at Schulz Bräu is like arriving at a happy German village. There is plenty of mixed seating available for up to 300 people outdoors with benches, tables, and chairs imported from Germany. Firepits burn through the cold seasons while shade trees and a misting system keep patrons cool during

Check the Schulz Bräu event page for information on Stammtisch–a German conversation group–Knoxville Storytellers, and Live Music, as well as Oktoberfest, Christkindlesmarket, and Maifest.

Left: Jäger schnitzel, sauerkraut, spätzle
Center: Dining hall
Right: Biergarten

spring and summer months. If the weather is uncooperative, guests can easily move indoors to the bierhall or upstairs to the mezzanine loft.

Order favorite German dishes at Schulzes Schnitzel Kitchen. Start with a pretzel with mustard and butter or add obatzda, a Bavarian cheese spread. Then try currywurst or fleischkäse, a German bologna loaf with sauteed onions.

The schnitzels, such as wiener schnitzel, are all made with pork, but have different toppings, like mushroom gravy or tomato sauce. Each schnitzel is served with choice of two with options like kase spätzle or sauerkraut.

Fun specialty pizzas at Schulz Bräu are inspired by German cuisine and popular combinations. Try a schnitzel pizza or go with the Bavarian knacker brat pizza. The Zeven, with pepperoni, pineapple, sweet corn, and feta cheese, is also good.

126 Bernard Ave., 865-415-3835
schulzesschnitzelkitchen.com

CENTRAL FILLING STATION

Tennessee's first full-service food truck park

You've heard the old adage—if you build it, they will come. Alden and Scott Larrick built Knoxville's first food truck park, and people came. Fashioned after an idea they had come across in other cities amid the trendy food truck craze, Central Filling Station opened in North Knoxville in 2018 in the perfect place—an old gas filling station site, complete with funky, vintage gas pumps.

Along came the picnic tables, then the bright blue umbrellas, a firepit, a covered seating area, and a bar with a selection of craft beers, seltzers, ciders, sodas, and even kombucha. The park has a specifically and intentionally sustainable design based on Alden's university studies. Drinks are available in aluminum cans for recycling. Old wooden spools serve as additional tables. A shipping container holds the bar.

Central Filling Station is family and pet friendly. Outdoor games are available for kids and grown-ups alike. Pets are allowed in the park but must be kept on a leash. Lunch and dinner service includes a rotating selection of up to four savory trucks along with one dessert truck scheduled to offer a diverse cuisine style at each meal. The park has hosted trucks specializing in Mexican, Italian, and Greek fare along with over 50 others featuring everything from burgers and hot dogs to ramen—and even flower trucks. Visit their website to view the monthly schedule and learn more about the participating trucks.

Exposure at the park has offered a few truck operators the opportunity to open dine-in restaurants around town—Fai Thai

One of the most popular activities for guests at Central Filling Station is writing their life pursuits on the "Before I die . . ." wall.

Top left: Bar at Central Filling Station

Top center: Choose from many food vendors

Top right: Longtime employees Lauren and Kaley

Bottom left: Dine in the park

Bottom right: Write a bucket list item on the "Before I die . . ." wall

and CJ's Tacos on Gay Street, and Penne for Your Thoughts in the Marble City Market food hall in the Regas Building. Oakwood BBQ also became the resident truck for Merchants of Beer in Knoxville's Old City.

Events at Central Filling Station have included a taco showdown, trivia, and live music. The park draws a crowd of locals and curious visitors who search for restaurants and entertainment during their stay. Street parking is available just outside the park.

The Larricks sold Central Filling Station to SMJT Real Estate Group in 2020 who kept the park open for the first time through the winter months for the purpose of offering outdoor seating space through the pandemic. Central Filling Station is open seven days a week during season. Fill 'er up!

900 N Central St., 865-333-4982
knoxfoodpark.com

THE OAK ROOM BY ABRIDGED

The Romance of Beer

Jesse Bowers and Joey Trott opened Abridged Beer Company in 2015 but soon after began looking for a space to create something somewhat different than their casual brewpub—an intimate aging and tasting room. In 2019, they found another off-the-beaten-path location in the "Happy Holler" area of Old North Knoxville, just off Central Street on Anderson Avenue. There, they opened the Oak Room.

Like most businesses in Old North Knoxville, you can find convenient parking right on the street near your destination. In the unique and cozy space, patrons eat and drink in the barrel room. You may find the Oak Room to be a perfect romantic date night venue. Linger over dinner, then walk right up the sidewalk to the quirky local movie theater, Central Cinema, where you might catch a showing of *Night of the Hunter*, the masterpiece with the screenplay by Knoxville's own Pulitzer Prize–winning James Agee. Or come early and shop for treasures of the past at Retrospect Vintage or Raven Records.

Upon entering the Oak Room, I know I might get a welcome wave as I glance back to the open kitchen where Chef Joey has entrusted the kitchen duties to Zach Jones. The base food menu at the Oak Room is Joey's, but Zach adds his own touches and specials.

A variety of flatbreads, toasted sandwiches, and mixed greens salads with "Anderson Gold" vinaigrette comprise the menu. Joey is particularly proud of the Oak Room Board featuring local ingredients like hand-selected meats and cheeses. You can also take on the whole Oak Room Experience—pair Joey's Oak Room Board with five-ounce samples of all eight of Jesse's barrel-aged sour beers.

Left: House flatbread

Center: The Oak Room on Anderson Avenue, just off Central Street

Right: Try a weekend special

The romance does not end in the physical setting of the Oak Room; it is only the beginning. While some guests will be interested in the combination of flavors and aging time of the beers, others will be fascinated with the names and stories, based on mythology, quotes, thoughts, and ideas. Artwork for the bottles is created by artist Amanda Fenner in her style of pointillism. Jesse and Joey have a real passion for food and drink, and they offer guests a unique, "romantic" experience in the Oak Room.

109 W Anderson Ave., 865-444-1949
abridgedoakroom.com

Jesse is especially excited about his new sour beer cocktail program. Stop by and see what he is creating!

ORIGINAL FREEZO

Historical gem of Happy Holler

There are many interesting and memorable sites along Central Street, but probably the most visually striking and unforgettable is the Original Freezo sign and building. Opened in 1947, this business has survived through many different developments in the area. From the prosperous times of the well-to-do residential neighborhood and nearby textile mills to the rough time of bars on all four corners of the so-called "Happy Holler" to the urban renewal and arrival of trendy restaurants, breweries, food trucks, coffee shops, event centers, and vintage shops, Freezo has seen it all.

Darrell Dalton has owned Original Freezo since 2001. Over the past 20 years, he has had the pleasure of welcoming guests back who frequented Freezo years ago and are surprised to return and find that it is still there, with the concrete tables and benches under the now-massive, white mulberry tree. Working in the refrigeration repair business, Darrell was already in the restaurant world, calling on eateries such as Dairy Queen, Sonic, Smoky Mountain Market, and eventually Original Freezo. When the owners were ready to sell, Darrell was ready to begin his new career.

After planning to demolish the first building and create a new restaurant with indoor seating, input from the public convinced Darrell that the community did not want that. The building features an old walk-in cooler and original floors and windows that have stood the test of time from the days of the streetcars. Darrell

> **Owner Darrell Dalton loves "the novelty of having a mom-and-pop shop that has withstood all the changes in the city and the world. We're still right here."**

Left: Order at the window

Center left: Owner Darrell Dalton and son Isiah

Center right: Look for the Freezo sign on Central Street

Right: Original Freezo sign, c. 1984. Courtesy Library of Congress

did add a drive-through window which has paid off, especially when the pandemic struck. Since customers were already used to using the drive-through, the pandemic did not have a huge impact on Original Freezo.

Business at Original Freezo is all about personalization. There is intentionally no speaker box for the drive-through, so employees can interact with guests. Darrell credits part of Freezo's success to the guests: "We've got good people."

Best sellers at Freezo are hot dogs, burgers, onion rings, ice cream, dipped cones, milkshakes, breakfast biscuits, frozen teas, and Mountain Dew. Homemade tamales are served in the winter for that Knoxville specialty dish, the Full House—tamales covered with chili.

There have been many offers from investors to buy the property, but Darrell hopes to one day pass the Original Freezo and its rich history on to someone who has the passion to keep it running for future generations to enjoy.

1305 N Central St., 865-637-6500

facebook.com/The-Original-Freezo-217765924982719

PIZZERIA NORA

A true taste of Italian

Although Pizzeria Nora opened in 2017, the business began in 2013 as a different concept many may remember as the North Corner Sandwich Shop. Amazing sandwiches were created there, and I would often bring one home to savor sitting outside on my porch. I remember when North Corner opened repeatedly hearing the phrase "chef driven." That chef is David Blevins.

David grew up in Huntsville, Alabama, but moved to Knoxville in 1975 for his father's job with the Tennessee Valley Authority. He later studied communications and marketing at the University of Tennessee and was employed in multiple different jobs including sales, retail, and publishing before attending culinary school at Johnson & Wales in Miami. After enjoying the opportunity to work as a chef in resorts in Colorado, Palm Beach, and the Caribbean, David decided to move back to Knoxville.

Having a fresh pasta company in the works as a farmers market business, David then came upon the building on Central that had been used as a commercial kitchen. The price was right, as the building needed some work, which David spent the next five to six months doing himself. His business background guided his decisions with determining food costs, finding good employees, and choosing what he considered a reliable enterprise of sandwiches rather than something trendy or too risky.

While David's sandwich shop was extremely popular, he wanted to move away from the lunch business to a concept with a more streamlined production. After procuring a used pizza oven, he set to work creating his Italian menu for his new "neighborhood hole-in-the-wall pizza joint": Pizzeria Nora, named after one of his favorite people, his mother.

Left: Owner and chef David Blevins and assistant Nick

Center: The panna cotta is a must-try

Right: Nick with fresh-baked pizza

At Pizzeria Nora, David has built a select menu featuring high-quality ingredients. Begin with one Consistent Salad—a Caesar topped with house-made croutons and dressing and freshly grated Parmesan. Choose from six pizzas or a daily special with traditional hand-pulled crust. Try the straightforward Margherita with house-made mozzarella, tomato, basil, and olive oil; the Nora Special featuring house-made sausage, goat cheese, and ricotta; or the Dino with molinari soppressata dry-cured salami and house-made sausage. End your meal with one amazing dessert—vanilla-buttermilk panna cotta with imported wild Italian cherries and pistachios.

Order for pickup or delivery Tuesday through Saturday, 5:30 p.m. to 8:30 p.m., through Slicelife, a service that specializes in independent pizzerias.

2400 N Central St., 423-737-0760
pizzerianora.com

One of David's fascinating jobs prior to becoming a chef was as a projectionist in a movie theater.

STEAMBOAT SANDWICHES

Right place at the right time

Central Street in Old North Knoxville is a fascinating voyage through a historic neighborhood, inventive eateries, craft breweries, coffee shops, bakeries, and vintage stores. If you make it through Happy Holler to the end of Central, you have arrived at your destination—Steamboat Sandwiches. Steamboat was created and opened by the Anderson family in 1989. For a while, they ventured into the heart of downtown with a shop on Market Square. After the Market Square stint, they were ready to move into other interests. Enter three enthusiastic entrepreneurs.

Matt Turner from Atlanta, Trevor Guydon of Miami, and Meredith Cole from Cleveland, Tennessee, had become friends while working downtown at Tomato Head. Between the three of them, they had accumulated a ton of restaurant experience. One chance evening while hanging out at Knoxville's popular Pecha Kucha—a Japanese-based storytelling platform for individuals to do a presentation of their work in a slideshow of 20 slides with 20 seconds of commentary per slide—they ran into friend John Sanders of Sanders Pace Architecture. John was going to be working on the old Steamboat Building and brought up the idea of someone taking over the sandwich shop. In 2017, the three friends began their journey as business owners.

While the pals weren't actively looking to start a business, they also "weren't not looking." They viewed owning a sandwich shop as a good opportunity and were excited to be part of an up-and-coming neighborhood that was in the midst of rebuilding and rebranding. Matt, Trevor, and Meredith also faced the challenges of entrepreneurship including working through an unexpected pandemic. An attractive space was created behind the building during this time for outdoor seating.

Top left: Dining room with historic photos

Top center: Sandwich with that famous Steamboat bread and potato salad

Top right: Red beans and rice

Bottom: Owners Trevor, Meredith, and Matt

The menu has remained basically the same. The Italian, the club, and the signature Steamboat—Genoa salami, ham, Swiss, and Exciter sauce—are the shop's best-selling sandwiches. Choose from two varieties of potato salad: loaded with a mayo base and tri-potato with a mustard base. Red beans and rice was an old Anderson family recipe that is still offered all year round. Hand-squeezed, shaken lemonade is a big seller.

The new owners love that their business is neighborhood driven. They focus on the community and everything local, including a garden across the street they work in. They are proud of keeping a long-standing business alive for the community. It just makes them feel good.

2423 N Central St., 865-444-1951
steamboatoncentral.com

The Andersons taught Matt, Trevor, and Meredith how to make their soft and shapely bread. Matt has the burn marks to prove it.

ALE'RÆ'S GASTRO PUB AND COFFEE BAR

A passion for food, music, and customer service

David Goldschmitt—he will also answer to Coach—began the Ale'Rae food truck with, and named for, his daughters Allie and Rachel in 2017. Their idea was always to work toward opening a stand-alone brick-and-mortar restaurant. In a quick four years, working through a pandemic, they made their dream happen. In November 2021, they opened Ale'Rae's Gastro Pub and Coffee Bar on Broadway in the former building of the Three Rivers Market food co-op.

The vintage two-story house became an extension of David's own house. During his 20-year career as a college-level soccer coach, he often had players over to his home for meals. The high degree of training for their sport required the student athletes to eat healthy, nutritious meals. David began researching and cooking those nourishing meals. Through this interaction, he also learned that some students were from homes experiencing financial hardships and would come by his house earlier for extra food. His outreach to students in this way also kept them off the streets and in a family-style environment. Some of David's students have become guests at Ale'Rae's and several have even come to work for him.

Just as passionate as David is about helping his students, he is equally passionate about the new Ale'Rae's location, food, music, and life in general. David knew he wanted to create a sense of intimacy in the space for guests and musicians. He designed the environment using reclaimed and recycled materials.

After building its following with the food truck, Ale'Rae's took right off at its opening. Rachel is a budding cook and her favorite

Left: New brunch items
Center: Owners Allie, David, and Rachel
Right: Dining room and stage for nightly live music

thing about the restaurant is working in the kitchen. Allie enjoys the business and administrative side. Additional to their flavorful food offerings, the family now has an additional offering for their guests—live music.

David kept the original food truck menu items such as tacos, burgers, and wraps as Ale'Rae's specialties, then added new entrees and "Best Friends," or sides. He notes that Best Friends are a very important part of the meal. A variation of his best-selling bacon butter bourbon burger is now available as bacon butter meatloaf. Grilled ribeye, pan-seared cod, blackened shrimp, Tuscan chicken, and barbecue pork round out the entrees but may change seasonally.

For David, food is emotional. His goal is to have guests trust him and walk away saying, "Wow!"

937 N Broadway, 865-924-2426
aleraes.live

David plans for an outdoor bar and beer garden at Ale'Rae's with cameras that will stream music from the inside stage.

RAMI'S CAFÉ

A restaurant family

Once upon a time, there were three brothers whose family was in the restaurant business. Their family sent them all off to college so that they could have other choices of enterprise besides working in restaurants. You might guess what happened next—they all wound up right back in the family business, with each of them operating their own eating establishment.

Basel Natour, who owns Rami's Café, is one of those brothers. His younger sibling, Bassam, operates Sami's Café on the west side of town and his older brother, Pete, runs Pete's in the downtown. Their father immigrated to the United States from Palestine and, with his brothers, owned the popular Copper Kettle and Helma's restaurants.

With a degree in economics, Basel spent some time working in retail management before opening Rami's Café in 2015. The café is named after the youngest of Basel's three sons, Rami, who was born with multiple disabilities. Basel is inspired and motivated by his family to work hard every day to make the business successful. He loves to hear Rami say, "How did everything go at Rami's Café today?"

A Southern-style breakfast and lunch of homemade dishes is served at Rami's on Monday through Saturday from 7 a.m. 'til 2:30 p.m. Having a breakfast and lunch service allows Basel more free time to be available for his family. It is the same model that Bassam and Pete use in their restaurants. Basel's mission is to provide a clean, consistent, and friendly environment with great customer service and affordable homemade food.

A popular choice for breakfast is Rami's breakfast special featuring two eggs your way, sausage or bacon and home fries, with toast or biscuit and gravy. Other options include breakfast sandwiches and biscuits; omelets filled with cheese, veggies, or meats; cinnamon

Left: Greek omelet, home fries, bacon, biscuits and gravy

Center: Owner Basel Natour

Right: The café's namesake, Rami

French toast; or a stack of three blueberry, chocolate chip, or pecan pancakes. For lunch, try Rami's jumbo burger, roast beef supreme, Philly cheesesteak, homemade chicken or tuna salad, a veggie wrap, or a customer favorite, the BLT.

The guests at Rami's include longtime neighborhood residents as well as young couples with children and families who have moved into the area. Basel enjoys working with neighborhood schools as part of his community outreach. Stop by and see how everything is going at Rami's Café today!

3553 N Broadway, 865-801-9067
ramiscafe.com

At Rami's Café, Basel Natour strives to create an enjoyable experience for his guests and bring them some happiness.

ALICE'S DINER

Mom-and-pop diner with family atmosphere

Just as a fancy, flamboyant restaurant can catch your attention, so can one with a very simple aesthetic. The stark white building on Broadway with just the word Restaurant on it instantly caught my attention. It is the home of Alice's Diner, run by Spring Kirby and Joey Janeway, their daughter Victoria, and their son Noah.

"I can have brown gravy on my potatoes and white gravy on my country fried steak? Well, let's do that." After Victoria helped me work out my meat and two lunch, she moved over and sat beside an elderly regular to assist him with his order, then discussed with another table what they would use their condiments for in order to bring out the right serving, creating a caring, personalized dining experience. How you want to eat is a priority at Alice's Diner. During the lean times of the pandemic, regulars kept the doors open by picking up meal kits to cook or heat at home.

Spring began working in her aunt and uncle's restaurant on Western Avenue when she was 14 years old. In 2013, she branched out and opened her own eatery, Spring's Country Kitchen on Rutledge Pike. Eventually in 2019, she bought the new restaurant and moved over to the much-more-prominent location on Broadway. She gained her cooking experience by working in the restaurant business and from watching and helping her grandmother in the kitchen.

> The remembrance of the sound of corn bread batter hitting a skillet and the smell of a meat loaf cooking in her grandmother's oven are inspirations to Spring Kirby.

Left: Spotless, diner-style seating
Center: Breakfast plate of scrambled eggs, sausage, bacon, hash brown, and toast
Right: Alice's Diner on Broadway

Some of Spring's best-selling dishes are a variety of burgers, chicken and dumplings, and a campfire chicken with potatoes, carrots, and corn cooked and served in a foil packet. Other daily specials might include fried catfish with hush puppies, Polish sausage with white beans, or seasoned fried okra. Or try a large bowl of pinto beans with corn bread or a classic club sandwich or a BLT. A variety of homemade desserts are available every day such as German chocolate, banana cream, pineapple upside down or hummingbird cakes, fruit cobblers, and pies.

Open from 6 a.m. to 3 p.m. on weekdays except Wednesday and 7 a.m. to 3 p.m. on weekends, breakfast is served all day at Alice's Diner, complete with omelets, egg sandwiches, biscuits and gravy, and more.

4405 N Broadway, 865-394-9396
facebook.com/alicesdiner865

THE ORIGINAL LOUIS' RESTAURANT

Old-school dining and service

Sure, you've been on Broadway, but have you been on Old Broadway? The purpose: experiencing some old-school Italian dining with Greek roots. The early 1900s saw a significant arrival of Greek immigrants into the United States and especially East Tennessee with its similar topography to some of the homeland. Knoxville benefitted greatly by way of many of the Greeks being involved in the restaurant business. Consistency, customer service, and a good value are Greek business attributes that Jimmy Brinias holds to standard at the Original Louis' Restaurant.

The Original Louis' Restaurant was opened in 1958 by Nick Chronis, Menas Keramidas, and Gus Peroulas. Chronis became full owner in 1973 after having a falling-out with his partners. Keramidas and Peroulas subsequently opened a competing restaurant right next door, calling it Louis' Inn. Hence, the Original Louis' name. In 1976, Chronis sold to Gus Brinias, who also owned Gus' Restaurant downtown. Gus and his son, Jimmy Brinias, strived to keep the Original Louis' as much the same as possible ever since. They weathered all the storms, including having to relocate a block away during the I-640 expansion, and the restaurant keeps loyal customers returning for the comfort of their familiar fare.

Guests can enjoy lunch specials of fresh calf liver, chicken parmigiana, fried flounder, or a veal cutlet served with two vegetables of the day, a tossed salad, and the choice of rolls, corn muffins, or garlic bread. Homemade Italian dishes of spaghetti with meatball, meat sauce, or sirloin steak as well as ravioli and lasagna are also available for lunch.

Left: Spacious dining room

Center left: Press for this long-standing restaurant

Center right: Chicken parmigiana, onion rings, garlic bread

Right: Wall murals

Dinner presents a larger menu selection including Louis' famous hand-breaded onion rings. Start with a Grecian salad or choose from a variety of sandwiches à la carte or hot steak, meatball, or pastrami sandwiches served with fries, onion rings, and a side salad. Italian house specialties include baked spaghetti, beef ravioli, manicotti, fettucini alfredo, and eggplant parmigiana. They also have selections like filet mignon, ribeye, or an extravagant seafood platter.

A banquet room is available for private dining and parties at Louis' with capacity of up to 60 guests.

4661 Old Broadway, 865-688-4121
theoriginallouis.com

Curbside service begins at 4 p.m. and includes salad, spaghetti, and lasagna pans, family packs of spaghetti, salad, and bread, and homemade meat sauce by the cup, pint, or gallon.

SAM & ANDY'S

A long-standing Knoxville tradition since 1946

"What are you having for dinner?" my friend asked over the phone. "Take out from Sam & Andy's," I responded. "I want some!" she said.

Sam and Andy Captain (an Americanized spelling of Kipatinopolos) immigrated to the United States from Greece in 1911. In the 1930s they operated a hat blocking shop on Market Street and later had a beer distributorship. The brothers then opened their eatery, the Tennessean, later simply known as Sam & Andy's, in 1946 at the corner of 18th Street and Cumberland Avenue on "The Strip" of the University of Tennessee's campus.

The Captains helped their nephews make it to America as well and had them help out and learn the restaurant business in the diner, which, like many restaurants of the time, was open 24 hours. As the family grew, they continued to open more restaurants around town to give the next generation jobs and opportunities.

Sam & Andy's continued in business serving their famous Vol Burgers and Steamed Sandwiches to the college crowd on Cumberland Avenue until 1997 when, much to the disappointment of generations of Knoxvillians, that location closed. The Farragut location on Kingston Pike continued, and there is also a location in Fountain City.

A Knoxville specialty, Sam & Andy's serves steamed sandwiches of smoked ham, turkey, corned beef, or as a Reuben, among others. Add a side of thick-cut, deep-fried onion rings or seasoned mushrooms.

That famous Vol Burger? It's made from certified Black Angus beef and cooked to your preference. As a testament to how much Knoxvillians love football, at Sam & Andy's you can have your choice of the Vol Burger, the Bacon Vol Burger, the Double Vol

Left: Sam & Andy's Fountain City

Center: Signature marinated and grilled chicken, fried okra, mashed potatoes and gravy

Right: Black Angus beef burger with fries

Burger, the Double Bacon Vol Burger, or live a little and go for the Tennessee Burger—a Vol Burger with both American and provolone cheese. It's a little-known fact the the Southeastern Conference (SEC) was created in a meeting at the Farragut Hotel on Knoxville's Gay Street in 1932. But burger fans will know that the SEC Burger was created at Sam & Andy's with hickory-smoked bacon, smoked cheddar cheese, topped with grilled onions.

While amazing sandwiches and burgers stand the test of time, these days a variety of fresh salads can also be found at Sam & Andy's. Try the signature homemade Parmesan ranch dressing and even purchase a bottle to take home!

2613 W Adair Dr., 865-281-9539
samandandysrestaurant.com

Call Sam & Andy's for daily specials of entrees with vegetables, pastas, and made-from-scratch desserts and cakes available by the slice or whole cakes.

INSKIP GRILL

Little place, big taste

Although the Inskip Grill first opened in 1967, it recently began to gain a revival of attention through local social media channels after new owner Justin Wiseman bought the classic eatery in 2018.

With a degree in criminal justice and after working in public safety and the corporate world, Justin decided it was time for him to make a career change into something he had become really good at: cooking.

Justin's culinary skills are self-taught and, like any good East Tennessean, from his grandmother. His focus is on creating unique flavors and taste combinations. After careful consideration of the old Inskip Grill menu, he decided what elements he could keep from the breakfast and country-style meat and vegetable plates to add to his modern outrageous burger and milkshake creations.

When the pandemic caused a shutdown almost overnight, Justin's wife, Karen, created a website with online ordering and takeout, but the tiny building on Inskip Road remained closed for indoor dining because of limited space to provide social distancing for guests. As a resident of the neighborhood, Justin quickly found his bigger space on Broadway. While he misses cooking at the bar of the original building and greeting and visiting with guests where he developed a loyal following, at the new space he has triple the indoor seating and additional outdoor seating. The dining room's gorilla mascot is a take on the nickname, "The Grilla," Justin's kids gave him.

The colossal burgers and sandwiches at Inskip Grill are made to order, crowned with unique toppings, and are named for local celebrities or landmarks. The Archie Campbell, named for the country music star with a spicy streak who got his start playing for a live radio show on Knoxville's Market Square, features a pepper

Left: Gorilla mascot on the Burgersphere

Center: The "Grilla" himself, Justin Wiseman

Right: Special burger with house-made chips

jack cheeseburger with bacon on jalapeno waffle bun. The Popcorn Sutton, named after the legendary local moonshiner, is a cheddar cheeseburger topped with moonshine-infused barbecue ham, bacon, and an onion ring. If your toppings don't include fried green tomatoes or mac and cheese, add a side for snacking.

In the Shakery, try a Grilla-sized massive shake such as the banana pudding shake, or a s'mores shake topped with, what else, marshmallows lit on fire.

4877 N Broadway, Ste. 5, 865-357-1554

inskipgrill.com

Justin would one day love to thank Joe Exotic, who was the inspiration for his Tiger King Burger–a half-pound patty, pimento cheese, Tiger Tenders, bacon, and grilled pineapples, served on Oklahoma Toast with an onion ring piercing–a best seller through the pandemic.

LITTON'S MARKET, RESTAURANT & BAKERY

Southern hospitality is the family business

Litton's celebrated Southern restaurant began its journey in 1946 when Eldridge Litton opened Litton's Market in the Inskip neighborhood in North Knoxville. The original market sold gas and carried a variety of groceries, produce, feed, and hardware. Eldridge's son Edwin became a partner in the business and by 1962 a deli counter had been added. The popularity of the 89-cent Litton Burger soon set the market in a new direction.

Edwin's son Barry became a butcher and opened a fresh meat market in Fountain City in 1980. He soon revived the Litton Burger and was taking counter orders. His sister Kelly studied at Rich's Cooking School in Atlanta with Nathalie Dupree and attended the Cordon Bleu Cooking School in London. Together they grew the meat market into a full-service restaurant. A bakery was added in 1983. Barry's son Erik attended Johnson & Wales in Charleston with plans to continue the family business.

At Litton's you might start out with a mixed greens salad, or just skip straight to the main event—those Litton Burgers. Thunder Road is an infamous nickname given to a route used by moonshiners from Harlan, Kentucky, to Maynardville, Tennessee, just north of Knoxville. It was the subject of Robert Mitchum's 1958 movie of the same name. At Litton's, Thunder Road is an infamous burger topped with pimento cheese, sauteed onions, and jalapeno. An Iowa premium beef steak sandwich as well as the trendy veggie burgers and an all-beef frank grilled chili dog are also available.

Left: Dessert case at Litton's
Center left: Italian cream cake
Center right: Litton's in Fountain City
Right: Carryout case

For lunch choose a daily meat and two plate with charbroiled chicken, fried schrod, turkey, or pork with your choice of two sides such as mashed potatoes or fresh-cooked greens.

Litton's Market To Go Menu includes pint-sized side items, entrees to heat and eat such as chicken and dumplings, pork barbecue, and broccoli casserole or meat to cook at home including a burger pack, chicken cordon bleu, and Norwegian kosher salmon.

Bakery desserts are a big hit at Litton's. Guests have a large selection of treats like cheesecakes, pies, cookies, and brownies. Products from the bakery can also be ordered online and shipped anywhere across the country.

2803 Essary Rd., 865-688-0429
littonsdirecttoyou.com

After corresponding to her inspiration Julia Child about her dream to become a chef, Kelly Litton received back a handwritten letter encouraging her to "Just do it."

THE AMBER RESTAURANT

Southern comfort cooking in a family-oriented environment

Remember when Barbara Mandrell sang that she was country when country wasn't cool? In Knoxville, there is a restaurant equivalent of that. The Amber Restaurant sits miles away from the hype of the trendy farm-to-table movement of downtown, but provides the simplicity of a timeless, down-home East Tennessee meal with its "ol'-fashion cookin'."

Longtime servers greet regular guests and wish them to "Have a good day!" and "Come back now!" as they leave. I considered my offer of "extra mayonnaise," and after seeing the ripe, locally grown tomato on my pimento cheese and bacon sandwich, it affirmed to me that this was a place operated by folks who care about what their guests eat.

Don and Bobbie Padgett opened this community favorite in 1977 but decided to retire during the shutdown for the pandemic. Former Amber grill cook Thomas DeBarros along with Knoxville native T. J. Eubanks bought the local favorite and continued with the same menu but added a few updates such as barbecue pulled pork. The Amber now accepts card payment and offers delivery, which has increased their business.

The Amber Restaurant offers breakfast every day from 7 a.m. until closing at 3 p.m. For lunch, a variety of salads are served with choice of house-made dressings. "We wouldn't use anything else," a longtime server informed me. The Amber Burger and hot and cold sandwiches, including a traditional fried bologna, are on the sandwich menu.

Thomas and T. J.'s loyal clientele return often for their favorite Southern comfort dishes such as pot roast, chicken and dumplings, and roast turkey with dressing and gravy. They also know that

Left: BLT with pimento cheese, fried okra

Center: Dining room and murals

Right: Sugar-cured ham with baked apples, deviled eggs, mashed potatoes, salad, cornbread muffin

every day, the Amber offers some dishes not commonly found in restaurants, such as chicken livers with onions and a Knoxville specialty, the Full House—a tamale smothered with chili. Daily specials include old-fashioned meatloaf, country-style steak, or homemade salmon patties.

The Amber's friendly staff won't let you forget about dessert. Choose chocolate or coconut meringue pie, strawberry or blackberry cobbler, or get decadent with a grilled honey bun topped with ice cream. One guest apologized profusely to those of us waiting in line to pay at the counter but when we found out she was trying to get a dessert to go, we completely understood. We were all thrilled and relieved for her when we heard a call from the kitchen, "I found you the last one!"

6715 Maynardville Pike, 865-922-7641
amberrestaurantknox.com

For fun, look for the Amber Restaurant on the Halls Crossroads-opoly version of the Monopoly board game.

SMILIN' JACK'S CAFÉ

A tribute café of three generations serving family recipes

If you never had the pleasure of meeting Smilin' Jack, you now have the opportunity to enter his world in the form of Smilin' Jack's Café, a tribute café. Who was Smilin' Jack? Tracy Hicks's daddy. Who is Tracy Hicks? When I first met Tracy, she was involved in a special program for Knox Area Rescue Ministries, which trained displaced people in the culinary arts and helped them find work cooking in local restaurants. Originally from Bristol, award-winning Tracy has been a general manager at some very high-profile hotel properties including the Martha Washington Inn & Spa for 10 years, the historic General Morgan Inn, Hilton Hotels Worldwide, Margaritaville Resort & Hotels, and most recently, the Embassy Suites in Downtown Knoxville.

When the pandemic began, Tracy decided to leave the hotel industry and live out her dream of the past 10 years of owning her own restaurant. After careful planning, the "Little Red Hen," as Smilin' Jack called her, opened her new venture in November 2020.

Knowing that Tracy pursues the highest-quality hospitality in her work, I was excited to find her new venture in Halls. Although professionally she has worked at some very upscale venues, her dream was to create a café with family, celebrating family, and using generational family recipes.

The menu of Smilin' Jack's features soups, sandwiches, salads, and burgers, all known by nicknames Smilin' Jack gave his family. Everything is made from scratch using fresh ingredients. A rotating variety of soups includes Jack's chili, creamy potato, and tomato basil. Sandwiches are served on a choice of three different kinds of fresh-baked bread and served with chips, or a side of house-made

Left: Steamed sandwich with pasta salad

Center: Homemade dessert case

Right: Little Red Hen panini, tomato basil soup

pasta, potato, or bacon pea salad. Try a panini like the best-selling Snowbird—roasted turkey, dried cranberries, swiss cheese, sliced Granny Smith apples, and blackberry jam—the E Dub Black Angus Burger or a Steamed JHaun French Dip. Choose a flatbread combination such as the bacon chicken ranch or meatball pesto or create your own.

Depending on the day, desserts might include a triple-layer chocolate or coconut cake, banana pudding, or a sugar pie made from a hundred-year-old recipe. Call ahead to take away a whole cake or pie. Soft drinks, lemonades, teas, and coffees with a multitude of choices of mix-ins continue the flavor adventure.

4620 Mill Branch Ln., 865-922-2227
smilinjackscafe.net

Smilin' Jack gave everyone he loved a nickname. For fun, ask who your dish was named after.

BURGER BOYS

Home of the free fries

Chapman Highway has generally been a sea of fast-food options and chain restaurants—until recently, when Jeffrey "Andre" Bryant opened his Burger Boys shop in 2018, right across from the major players, McDonald's and Wendy's. That type of competition doesn't intimidate Andre at all; in fact, he seems to relish it. You see, Andre trained and worked in quick-service restaurants for 35 years. Now, he takes on the biggest in the business and beats them at their own game.

Andre began his career as a teenager working at Wendy's in Columbus, Ohio. Of course, there is the famous Knoxville–Wendy's connection. Wendy's founder, Dave Thomas, also began his career as a teenager, working in Knoxville at the Regas Restaurant and becoming best friends with Bill Regas as they made sandwiches together for workers heading to the secret city of Oak Ridge. When Dave's family decided to move, George Regas told him to come back anytime and they would have a job for him. Dave replied that he was going to have many restaurants of his own someday. Wendy's grew to be the second-largest fast-food franchise.

His hard work paid off, and by the time Andre graduated from high school, he had been promoted to store manager. Working his way up through the ranks of Wendy's, he eventually became the lead of the franchise training program for one of the largest Wendy's franchises in the country. Studying the Wendy's business model, Andre became interested in opening his own restaurant.

In Andre's corner he has quality product: big, juicy, and never-frozen burgers; the freshest toppings; good value; first-rate customer service; and, of course, free fries with every burger. His building is drive-through only, eliminating the need for a big staff while keeping customers safe during the pandemic.

Left: Hand-painted murals
Center: All burgers come with free fries
Right: Burger Boys drive-through

Burger Boys burgers are named for Andre's sons and are all a half pound except for the Big Dom, which is a full pound with habanera sauce, cayenne sauce, jalapenos, tomato, and lettuce. The Kobe, Lil Dom, Lil Dre, Dante, and Sasha come with a variety of different toppings, or the Vol Burger is created according to guests' preferences.

Livers and gizzards, oh my! In addition to burgers, Andre also has Southern favorites available like fried chicken sandwiches and catfish. Desserts include cheesecake and sweet potato pie.

2400 Chapman Hwy., 865-577-1705
myburgerboys.com

Visit Burger Boys 11 a.m. to 6 p.m., Monday through Saturday.

YE OLDE STEAK HOUSE

Family owned since 1968

Do you want a steak? I mean, do you want a steak? Then head out on busy Chapman Highway to the iconic Ye Olde Steak House for old-school flame-grilled goodness. Don't blink rounding a curve, or you are likely to miss the rustic log cabin–style building tucked back at the base of a steep hillside. Park and walk down for a filling dinner, then catch a provided ride back up to your vehicle.

Bunt King was a businessman who wanted to open a family-style restaurant. One day in 1968, he went home and announced to his wife, Helen, that he had found the perfect location: a former antique store in South Knoxville. It took some convincing, but eventually Helen and other extended family decided to back Bunt and his plan for a steak house. The Kings began a tradition of serving the best grain-fed Iowa beef. Many satisfied customers later, Ye Olde Steak House is still going strong. Bunt passed away in 1987, and Helen in 2003, but their children Nancy Ayres, Cheryl Wilson, and David King have continued the tradition.

Your meal will begin with complimentary crackers and spreadable cheese. Add a chilled shrimp cocktail, golden onion rings, or battered button mushrooms. All steaks are served with a salad and choice of side such as steamed broccoli or best-selling woodshed fried potatoes. Diners can enjoy various cuts of meat and proteins ranging from New York strips to stuffed flounder.

For dessert, treat yourself to house-made pie or cake. Miss Ethel, who has been baking at Ye Olde Steak House for 43 years, heads up the dessert team, making pies like key lime and peanut and cakes like German chocolate and coconut. Whole desserts are also available but must be ordered one day in advance.

Top left: Ye Olde Steak House on Chapman Highway

Top right: House salad

Bottom left: Beef tenderloin filet, broccoli casserole, woodshed potatoes

Bottom right: House-made desserts since 1968

While a good steak can be pricey, guests can also partake in Ye Olde Steak House's early bird and nightly specials. Monday is burger night with one side, while the Wednesday special is a grilled chicken sandwich with one side or chicken dinner with two sides. Monday through Thursday early bird specials are offered 4 to 6 p.m.

6838 Chapman Hwy., 865-577-9328
yeoldesteakhouse.com

Ye Olde Steak House has for many years been recognized as the best steak house in Knoxville. Check out the *Man v. Food* Knoxville episode where Adam Richman takes on a 60-ounce New York strip!

SOKNO TACO CANTINA

A gem in the wilderness

For much of its existence, South Knoxville was viewed by many as separate from the rest of the city, separated literally by the Tennessee River. While multimillion-dollar businesses operated just across the Gay Street Bridge, South Knoxville remained quiet and unassuming. Eventually, just as downtown's abandoned buildings were revived to be showcased as Knoxville's crown jewels, South Knoxville's unaffected beauty is now showcased as its natural treasure. With the creation of Knoxville's Urban Wilderness, locals and visitors can escape to 1,000 wooded acres along the waterfront, including 50 miles of hiking and biking trails, 10 parks, and four virtually untouched Civil War forts. "SoKno" had arrived. But outdoor recreation requires much sustenance. Enter Bryan "Howie" Howington's SoKno Taco Cantina, located just outside Baker Creek Preserve.

Since 2017, SoKno Taco has served tasty dishes and accompaniments with made-from-scratch seasonings and sauces. Entrees such as beef or chicken tamales are served with cast iron beans and fiesta rice or black bean salad and chips with guests' choice of pico de gallo or fire-roasted tomato, tomatillo, or habanero salsa. Breakfast burritos and taco lunch specials are offered every day from 11 a.m. until 3 p.m. and they even have vegan, vegetarian, and gluten-free entree options!

Happy Hour is daily from 4 to 7 p.m. and all day Sunday. Smart mocktails provide something special for everyone and are included in the happy hour specials. SoKno Taco enjoys working with area schools and community organizations, and they partner with local breweries to host a monthly SoKno Social, with a designated charity receiving a portion of the proceeds of the event.

Left: Outdoor patio
Center left: Dining room
Center right: Burrito platter
Right: Modern decor at SoKno Taco

In addition to SoKno Taco, Howie also operates Cool Beans Bar & Grill on the UT Campus and, in 2012, opened Central Flats & Taps on the north side of town. Flats & Taps was one of the first businesses that helped revitalize Happy Holler and Old North Knoxville. A successful concept for Flats & Taps was utilizing ingredients that could be used in multiple dishes. Specialties include dips and hummus, wings, soups, salads, wraps, paninis, pastas such as lasagna and ravioli, and 12 varieties of stone-baked flatbreads. Two additional flatbreads benefit the Legacy Parks Foundation with one dollar per flat donated to the organization.

3701 Sevierville Pike, 865-851-8882
soknota.co

Plan a road trip to Johnson City to visit Howie's other concepts: Holy Taco Cantina and Tipton Street Pub!

LANDING HOUSE

Chinese, Cambodian, and French inspired

For the past many years, Sevier Avenue was a road less traveled, an industrial area that led to the sleepy neighborhood of Island Home and the Ijams Nature Center, one of the most peaceful destinations in Knoxville. The nature center was the property of Harry (H. P.) and Alice Ijams. Typical East Tennesseans, they were interested in natural surroundings, outdoor life, and adventure, even spending their honeymoon hiking through the Smoky Mountains. H. P. was a commercial artist, illustrator, and an ornithologist. He studied birds, and used the Ijams property as a bird sanctuary. Alice grew flowers to supply florist shops and to sell to the public at the Market House downtown. After H. P. and Alice's passing, their daughter proposed the idea of preserving the property as a public park. In 1966, the City of Knoxville purchased their land and dedicated Ijams Nature Park in 1968.

Many trendy new businesses have sprung up along Sevier over the past few years. There is now a coffee shop, a pizza joint, some beer joints, a smoothie joint, a food truck park, and a "Simpl" restaurant, as well as new-construction upscale condos and apartment buildings. Zach and Hao Land opened their Asian fusion Landing House restaurant in a century-old two-story house. The second time I went back, I kept looking for the parking lot where I parked the first time, finally realizing a condo development had sprung up in the same spot.

At the Landing House, spend some time admiring the lovely, restored home, or take a covered seat on the spacious lawn. Begin your meal with my favorite, Thai iced tea, and some small plates of spring rolls, tom yum pork rinds, or fried tofu and eggplant.

Left: Landing House on Sevier Avenue
Center left: Fried rice and Thai iced tea
Center right: Bar area
Right: Coconut cheesecakes with variety of toppings

Unique entrees include gai lan (charred Chinese broccoli with hot honey mustard and a garlic confit glaze) or salaw machew (a braised beef dish with butternut squash and glass noodles). Try the madras curry with carrots, green peas, fried potatoes, bamboo shoots, and roasted red peppers.

Fried or steamed rice combos are available and also half price during happy hour, all day Monday and Wednesday, Thursday, and Sunday from 4 p.m. until 6 p.m. Kuy teav, or cambadian pho combos, might contain sous vide beef brisket, chicken, or shrimp.

1147 Sevier Ave., 865-249-7424
landinghouse-109226.square.site

After lunch or dinner, take a leisurely walk behind Landing House to the beautiful new waterfront, seven-acre Suttree Landing Park along the Tennessee River.

GUS'S GOOD TIMES DELI

Keeping a tradition

Gus Captain opened his Good Times Deli near campus on March 13, 1981. It soon became a staple of the University of Tennessee experience where students, alumni, and even visiting celebrities can enjoy a satisfying meal together. Although Gus retired in 2003, he left the deli in capable hands with Aaron Hale, who joined him in 1993. To the delight of their customers, Aaron has kept everything basically the same.

Price-conscious daily specials of a burger or sandwich with fries and a drink appeal to Gus's primary clientele, college kids. Some guests are even third-generation customers mixed with the older folks looking for a taste of nostalgia. Along a street full of corporate chains, patrons are happy to search out and support a small, local eatery. Aaron knows the usual orders of regulars when they walk in the door.

Appetizers, snacks, and starters include dishes like fried pickles and cheese bings, which are two types of deep-fried cheese traditionally served with ranch dressing. Or go healthy with a chef, chicken, or Greek salad.

Those famous Knoxville steamed sandwiches are part of the menu. Long ago, when fresh bread was not always available, industrious East Tennesseans implemented a way to soften bread for their sandwiches. The idea of the steamed sandwich caught on all around

Musician Garth Brooks became an avid supporter of Gus's, despite Aaron refusing to sell him beer one night when the singer came in after 3 a.m.

Left: Celebrity and sports star memorabilia

Center: Hot deli sandwich, fries, and cheese bings with ranch

Right: University of Tennessee–themed dining room

town. At Gus's, you can choose from a Reuben, a ham and salami hoagie, or build your own with a variety of choices.

Other favorites include the eight-ounce grilled fresh burger, chicken parmesan, barbecue beef, fried flounder, lamb and beef or chicken gyro, and a Philly steak and cheese. Or choose a comforting BLT, hot dog, or grilled ham and cheese.

Aaron steered Gus's through the pandemic to celebrate their 40th year in business. Those wild collegiate hours of open 'til 4 a.m.? Since the pandemic they've cut down a little, to about 2 a.m.

815 Melrose Pl., 865-525-9485
facebook.com/gusgoodtimesdeli

SALOON 16

Showcasing "The Sheriff"

Many visitors to Knoxville are especially interested in college football. Knoxvillians take college football to heart. Consider checking out the old Farragut Hotel on Gay Street. A plaque outside the circa-1919 building commemorates the creation of the SEC, the Southeastern Conference, in 1932. Take Gay Street to Cumberland Avenue and straight down to the University of Tennessee to view Neyland Stadium, the seventh-largest sports stadium in the world. Then head over to a unique football-related dining experience inside the Graduate Hotel, Saloon 16.

At the Graduate Hotel, guests enter a Southern preppy aesthetic—nautical (the front desk is a small boat—think Vol Navy) plaid (Tennessee orange and white, of course), antique tables, bamboo chairs, oversize tabletop books, and a dash of velvet. Graduate Hotels is a concept by UT alum Ben Weprin. The boutique hotels are centered around university towns and celebrate their collegiate culture. There are currently 30 locations in the US and two in the UK with two more in the works. One of Ben's investors in the Knoxville property is another UT alum, Peyton Manning, a.k.a. "The Sheriff."

You've heard that phrase, "Business in the front, party in the back." In the lobby of the Graduate Hotel, you might check your family in for the weekend, schedule a tour of the UT campus, or arrange a coffee meeting. But move on toward the back of the hotel for the party at Peyton's Saloon 16, his restaurant and bar that highlights the football career of the Pro Football Hall of Fame member.

Saloon 16 is filled with Peyton's personal memorabilia and photos, and the jukebox is loaded with his selections. Dark wood and a large mural keep with the western theme. A small stage hosts live music, and surprise musical guests have included Morgan Wallen and Eric Church.

Left: Barbecue dinner special, cheese bings with salsa and ranch

Top center: Stage for live music

Top right: Zane and Creed's mac & cheese

Bottom Center: Sloppy Joe with crinkle fries

Bottom right: Mural featuring the Sheriff

Have fun with the bar bites and cocktails, discovering their namesakes—people and sports figures of Knoxville or inspired by Peyton's time at UT. Choose between John Ward's loaded cheese fries or the legendary cheese bings; how to decide? Or go healthy with Condredge's (Holloway) Cobb salad or more substantial with the Graduate burger, Faye's (Julian) shrimp & grits or Peyton's chicken parm sandwich. Beloved women's basketball coach Pat Summitt's Royal Sprite tops the cocktail list or guests can choose from Ye Olde Wine List—red or white. Enjoy Peyton's addition to Knoxville's dining scene!

1706 Cumberland Ave., 865-437-5500
graduatehotels.com/knoxville/restaurant/saloon-16

Although it opened in the midst of the pandemic in August 2020, Saloon 16 boasts up to a three-hour wait on game days.

COPPER CELLAR

The answer is always yes

I once glanced around and saw a sign behind a bar at Copper Cellar that said, "The answer is always yes," challenging employees to create the best experience for their guests. I like that. Providing fantastic customer service has led to much success for restaurateur Mike Chase's Copper Cellar family of restaurants since 1975.

The original location, off busy Cumberland Avenue, features designated parking behind the building. In the evenings, you might want to hide away and dine downstairs, or "Down in the Cellar." Rich wood, leather, and Tennessee marble add to the luxurious feel of the space. Get decadent with prime rib, a bleu cheese sirloin, New York strip, or filet mignon.

Distinct features and workmanship continue upstairs with a collection of chandeliers, cut and stained-glass windows, oak cabinetry, and the elevated bar in the center of the restaurant. Enjoy casual dining with something for everyone, such as a wide selection of salads including the Volunteer Country with ham, fried chicken, and bacon and your choice of house-made dressings. You can also build your own burger, with lots of options to choose from.

Copper Cellar West is located at 7316 Kingston Pike near West Town Mall. It offers the same great dishes as the original location and the brunch of your dreams. On Sundays from 10 a.m. to 2 p.m., an entire room is dedicated to brunch offerings including made-to-order waffles, omelets, carved prime rib, and a dessert

> The first cappuccino machine in Knoxville was ordered from Italy for the Copper Cellar restaurant.

Left: Original Cumberland Avenue location

Center: Stuffed mushrooms special

Right: Dining room filled with rich wood and chandeliers

station. It is an amazing variety at a great value. There is often a wait for seating but tables in the bar area are first come, first served.

The other side of the same building houses Copper Cellar's take on Italian cuisine, Cappuccino's, opened in 1977. The menu of Cappuccino's is based on generational recipes from the Sicilian-Italian family of Chef Frank Aloise. You can also enjoy antipasti of Mamma's meatballs, arancini, fried ravioli, or fresh jumbo scallops.

1807 Cumberland Ave., 865-673-3411
coppercellar.com

SUNSPOT

Where tie-dyes and neckties unite

"**D**o you remember the first Sunspot?" someone recently asked me. Sunspot was a unique concept offering a mix of Caribbean, Southwestern, and healthy dining options created by Kelly Henderson near the UT campus. Eventually it changed ownership to Randy Burleson, who already had success in the restaurant business with his daughter's namesake, Aubrey's. I remember laughing when Randy noted Sunspot was his employees' favorite restaurant—especially the girls—as I had brunch there every Sunday.

Randy was always the hardest worker in the restaurant—running food, clearing tables, wrapping utensils, and taking care of any detail that needed attention. I learned that Randy was investing in iconic Knoxville restaurants that needed some care, and I thought that was a very cool idea. This included another staple of Cumberland Avenue, Stefanos Pizza.

Sunspot also achieved much success, led by Randy's work ethic as an example to his team. It has been consistently voted by locals as Best Vegetarian and Best Lunch and Brunch Spot. By 2013, it became necessary to expand to a larger location, just down the street. R2R Design Studio, a Knoxville-based architectural firm specializing in restaurant design, took on the task of combining three buildings for the new eatery.

Start with the traditional Sunspot tomatillo or smokey chipotle salsa with chips. Choose a healthy kale and quinoa salad or seasonal hummus. Other options include blackened shrimp or seared salmon tacos and sandwiches like black bean burgers and tofu melts. Entrees are rice or grain bowls, pasta, herb-roasted chicken, salmon with a grit cake, or even an omelet of the week.

Left: Roasted carnitas sandwich, black beans, chips with guacamole and two kinds of salsa

Center: New Sunspot location on Cumberland Avenue

Right: Brunch waffle special with bacon, eggs, and fried potatoes

Their brunch is incredible, too, and you can try delectable specials such as key lime pie waffles—key lime curd, whipped mascarpone, graham cracker crumbs, and candied lime—or other brunch favorites like biscuits and gravy or overnight French toast.

In 2015, Randy added a new concept to his campus-area portfolio—Fieldhouse Social in the University Commons. Part sleek-and-stylish sports bar, part man cave, here you can watch a game or attend a trivia night while enjoying one of their delicious burgers.

2200 Cumberland Ave., 865-637-4663
sunspotrestaurant.com

Check out a fun feature of Fieldhouse Social: the "Largest TV in the Southland."

PLAID APRON

Community-focused, made-from-scratch cuisine

If you want to plan a beautiful day out in Knoxville, it might involve a drive through the distinctive Sequoyah Hills neighborhood. Throughout this upscale community, you can view stunning homes in many different design styles including English cottage, American Colonial, Tudor Revival, neoclassical, Spanish, and midcentury modern, among others. Drive along the Tennessee River, view Papoose Park and Panther Fountain with their Cherokee and Art Deco influences, and stop for a refreshing meal at Plaid Apron.

The Plaid Apron was opened in 2011 by Chef Drew McDonald and his wife Bonni. Drew obtained degrees in food systems management from Lipscomb University in Nashville and culinary arts from Sullivan University in Louisville. He spent time working at Blackberry Farm before traveling to and cooking in New Zealand. He later returned to Tennessee and joined the team at the Capitol Grille at the Hermitage Hotel in Nashville. After moving back to Knoxville, Drew and Bonni had a goal of opening a restaurant focused on community, local farmers and producers, and Chef Drew's original cuisine.

Hours at the Plaid Apron are Wednesday through Sunday, with brunch from 9 a.m. until 2 p.m., and dinner from 5 p.m. to 9 p.m. Breakfast offers choices like a sausage or veggie omelet, a grits-and-vegetable hash, and gluten-free almond cakes with strawberries and maple syrup.

Lunch fare includes a farmers plate, a market salad with shaved vegetables, and kale salad with avocado and sweet potatoes, as well as heartier options like a catfish sandwich or grilled cheese. Add a side of fresh fruit or tomato soup.

Left: Plaid Apron in Sequoyah Hills

Center: Brunch patty melt with taters and fresh fruit

Right: Open dining room

The Plaid Apron is a popular dinner destination, so make your reservations far in advance. Can you have breakfast for dinner at the Plaid Apron? Well, sure! Choose between omelets, French toast, and more. There is a variety of crudite, bread with salted butter and radish almond pesto, and a dish that immediately catches my eye—milky bread soup—patterned, no doubt, after the Appalachian tradition of soaking corn bread in milk. Enjoy a burger, fish or pasta entree, a meat and plate, or one of Chef Drew's specials for the evening.

1210 Kenesaw Ave., 865-247-4640
theplaidapron.co

At the Plaid Apron, they note that everything is made from scratch except the hot sauce and the ketchup. Oh, and yes, plaid aprons are part of the attire!

HARD KNOX PIZZERIA

Neo Neapolitan pizza that packs a punch

Alexa Sponica is a lady on a mission: to reintroduce area neighborhoods to old-world culinary methods through modern concepts, namely through the crispy crunch of neo Neapolitan Pizza. Hard Knox Pizzeria set up shop in the Bearden District in 2009, but Alexa bought the majority share of the concept in 2014. She quickly implemented one of her other missions—the School of Hard Knox, a program to connect local communities and underresourced schools with local chefs to give food service exposure and provide future opportunities and careers for youth. Her diligence with this program helped earn Alexa a spot in Knox Biz's Top 40 Under 40.

Alexa's core values in business are: everything matters, living the Golden Rule, keep it real, going 11, love of craftmanship, loving the community, and figuring it out. She also stresses treating others with dignity and respect.

In 2017, Hard Knox expanded its Bearden location to double the size while keeping its original boxing theme. In 2018, Alexa's team opened a second location in Hardin Valley at 10847 Hardin Valley Road. They are excited to be opening a third location in 2022 at 2300 North Central Street beside the upcoming Ebony & Ivory Brewing and will take food orders from nearby Elst Brewing Company.

Want to impress your friends? Have the Hard Knox Mobile Pizza Oven at your next event!

Left: Expanded dining room at original location

Top center: Combination of four best-selling pizzas

Bottom center: Monthly special pizza

Right: Wood-fired oven

Swing by Hard Knox for a lunch special of an eight-inch wood-fired pizza, a half salad, and a fountain drink. Have your family or friends with you? Hard Knox also offers all their red and white pies in 12-inch versions. So what's it gonna be? Their Rocky Balboa and Iron Mike pizzas are most popular, but beyond pizza, guests might choose anything from mini meaballs to house-made focaccia with Parmesan and fresh rosemary. Try a calzone and end the night with a root beer float, sweet s'mores pizza, or dessert knots in seasonal flavors.

4437 Kingston Pike, 865-602-2114
hardknoxpizza.com

RED ONION

Pizza, subs, and Indian cuisine

At one time, the University of Tennessee had graduate and married student apartments on Sutherland Avenue. Students from many different countries were key to the street developing with many diverse food options. Along Sutherland you can find Mediterranean, Middle Eastern, Ethiopian, and Italian fare, an Oriental Super Mart, and a quaint mom-and-pop shop serving pizza alongside Indian cuisine. The first time I saw the sign for Red Onion Pizza and Indian food, I was immediately intrigued. What's that all about?

Shahid Masood immigrated to Knoxville from Pakistan in 1977. He and his wife, Saira, opened the Red Onion in 1989, in the same building where they are still located. Shahid wanted to open a pizza place, while Saira wanted to do Indian food, so they simply decided to combine the two. The two developed a loyal following of customers over the years as everyone in the area came to know them. Shahid noted that many business owners on Sutherland are friends, and some even opened their restaurants around the same time as the Red Onion.

Many guests order takeout from the Red Onion, but they do not offer delivery. Shahid and Saira have a comfortable business. Their children are grown and on their own (one is a doctor and one a lawyer) but Shahid wants to run the restaurant as long as possible. "I don't want to sit at home!" he insists. Red Onion offers reasonable prices for their guests because, as Shahid says, "You can't take it with you."

At Red Onion, you can start with breadsticks with a zesty red sauce or garlic cheese sticks. Try a three-cheese, meatball, or chicken calzone or a stromboli with your choice of fillings. You can

Left: Owners Shahid and Saira Masood

Center: Mediterranean pizza

Right: Red Onion on Sutherland Avenue, open until 8 p.m.

also try their antipasti or variety of sub sandwiches.

Their best-selling pizzas are the herbs and spice, Mediterranean, the Colossal, and the Meaty Deluxe featuring pepperoni, beef, bacon, ham, and sausage, and tasty Indian favorites include tandoori chicken, beef curry, and lamb biryani. For dessert have the homemade baklava. Red Onion is open Monday through Saturday from 11 a.m. until 8 p.m. Get to know Shahid and Saira!

3625 Sutherland Ave., 865-584-7445
redonionpizzas.com

Vegetables are fresh and hand-cut and their dough and sauce are made from scratch every day!

GOSH ETHIOPIAN

Fun and romantic

I had heard about Gosh Ethiopian Restaurant long before I ever went there to eat. Or should I say, long before I ever got up the nerve to go there to eat. Sometimes we feel hesitant to experience something new. But everyone who told me about Gosh raved about how good it was. So I definitely wanted to try it out.

Gosh is located on Sutherland Avenue, along the area where many international restaurants developed when the University of Tennessee had their graduate and married student housing across the street. I love these small, intimate eateries that have a romantic feel to them. Walking into Gosh, I didn't even know what to expect. Guests are greeted with modern wooden floors, white tablecloths, relaxing colors, a serene atmosphere, an attentive staff, and a sense of respect. I immediately loved it.

It's like they say, if you are unsure about what to order, just ask. The staff at Gosh is very helpful with describing their menu items. Yes, the dishes are served with injera, the traditional Ethiopian flatbread meant to be used to scoop food in place of utensils. That's all part of the fun of this dining experience. Injera is a sour fermented bread. It's a bit spongy and a bit moist. I had, by chance, ordered a tea that came with a spoon, which helped me out until I got a grasp on scooping.

Begin your meal at Gosh with an Ethiopian spiced hot or iced tea, or coffee. Slow-cooked meat, lentil, and vegetable stews are prepared fresh daily. The food is spicy—not in a burn-your-mouth sort of way, but in a clear-your-head sort of way.

Although the names are different, you'll find many of the ingredients to be familiar. Kay Wot is lean chopped beef simmered in

Left: Combination platter of meats and veggies
Center: White tablecloth dining room
Right: Relax with an Ethiopian tea

a hot pepper sauce with Ethiopian spices while Alicha Wot is beef in a mild sauce with ginger, curry, and garlic. Vegetable dishes include red lentils, yellow peas, cabbage, mushrooms, and collard greens. Dessert is baklava or cake with dates, pecans, and brandy sauce.

3609 Sutherland Ave., 865-544-4475
goshethiopian.net

Sharing a platter at Gosh with friends or a date is a fun and interactive night out. Visit them Wednesday through Friday from 5 p.m. until 8 p.m. and Saturdays, 4 p.m. until 8 p.m.

LONG'S DRUGSTORE & FOUNTAIN

Where time slows down

The story of Long's begins in the 1950s when folks from White Stores Grocery approached pharmacist Clarence Long with the idea of opening a drugstore in Knoxville's first shopping center. In 1956, Clarence took on the challenge with fellow pharmacist John Benson. By 1959, Jim Peck came on board as the third pharmacist at Long's. When Dr. Long passed away in the mid-1960s, his wife sold the business to Jim and his brother Ed. Jim's son, Hank Peck, now runs Long's. His sister, wife, and children have all worked at Long's over the years.

Long's is more than just a pharmacy or drugstore. It has become a neighborhood gathering place with members of the community stopping into the soda fountain for breakfast meetings, lunch dates, and afternoon snacks.

Opening at 8 a.m., Long's breakfast is served all day except for pancakes, French toast, and omelets served until 11 a.m. Have a Rise & Shine Biscuit Breakfast with two eggs, bacon or sausage, and a biscuit with gravy. Go all out with Long's Southern Breakfast—two eggs, chuckwagon steak or fried chicken patty smothered in gravy, grits, and toast with butter and jelly.

Show up early for the French toast breakfast with bacon or sausage, Long's three-egg steak or Southwestern omelet, or a Smoky Mountain pancake breakfast. Choose a Pride of the Southland for one specialty pancake, two eggs, bacon or sausage, and grits.

A salad plate includes one scoop of cottage cheese, egg salad, and tuna salad, with sliced peaches, but you can also have any of those

Left: Long's Drugstore & Fountain on Kingston Pike

Center: Hand-dipped milkshakes and floats

Right: Long's burger and seasoned fries

or chicken salad as a stuffed tomato. Purchase salads or pimento cheese by the pint to take home.

More of Long's mainstays are their hand-dipped milkshakes, malts, and floats in many different flavors. What will you choose— cherry vanilla, chocolate peanut butter, mint chocolate chip, or jamocha? Local Mayfield Ice Cream is available by the bowl or cone or go ahead and have the banana split!

4604 Kingston Pike, 865-588-9218
ldsknox.com

Pick up some UT merchandise or gifts and greeting cards while at Long's!

FARMACY

Eat your heart out

When you enter Farmacy, you immediately notice the decor. It is a very pretty and feminine space, light and open, with hints of linen and lattice. You'll also notice the beautiful presentation of the food. This attention to detail may come from owner Bettina Hamblin's catering background. In 2008, she began her Luxe Catering business, providing lovely settings for weddings, parties, and various private dining events. Bettina loves being creative, and she is constantly seeking out fresh new ideas for food and decor.

By 2017, Bettina decided to open Farmacy, her restaurant on Northshore near Pellissippi. It was a small space, but she made it work, and the eatery grew in popularity. She was soon in need of a larger place, eventually even searching around town with mentors Grady and Bill Regas for the perfect new space. In 2020, Bettina moved Farmacy to a much larger building in Bearden and has been embraced by the community.

Farmacy features Southern favorites with a bright, modern twist. The focus is on providing freshly prepared made-from-scratch meals using ingredients from local purveyors. Some suppliers to Farmacy include Painted Hills Beef, Shelton Farms, Sweet Water Valley Cheese, Sunrise Dairy, and Flour Head Bakery.

Lunch features many healthy options like vitality and enlightened bowls—or you can indulge with the Farmacy burger or Good Ole Boy brisket French dip with white cheddar and au jus. For dinner, larger dishes are available as well, such as lemon rosemary chicken, and a bone-in pork chop with roasted acorn squash.

If you can't save room for dessert, just order one to take home for later. Sweets include strawberry cake and blackberry sage shortcake with sage custard and fried biscuit.

Top left: Welcome—Eat your heart out!

Top center: Good Ole Boy French dip

Top right: Farmacy dining room

Bottom left: Dave's eggs for Saturday or Sunday brunch

Bottom *center:* Happy hour specials—hot chicken, mac & cheese, cornbread

Bottom right: Brussels sprouts with bacon, pears, and pepper jelly vinaigrette

Enjoy a leisurely brunch Saturdays from 10 a.m. to 3 p.m. and Sundays 10 a.m. to 4 p.m. with local eggs and thick-cut bacon, biscuits and gravy topped with fried chicken, a breakfast burrito, Southern fried tofu, avocado toast, or churro waffles.

Reservations and curbside pickup are available at Farmacy!

5018 Kingston Pike, 865-247-4678
knoxfarmacy.com

Farmacy features some of the best happy hour specials Monday through Friday from 4 p.m. to 6 p.m. with half-price appetizers, $3 tacos, and $8 hot chicken.

UNION PLACE BAR & GRILL

This must be the place

Husband and wife team Aaron and Jenn Nelson arrived in Knoxville in 1996 and began working in and managing local bars and restaurants such as the Old College Inn, the Half Barrel, and Boyd's Jig & Reel. Finally, in 2017, they took over as owners of Union Jack's English Pub on Northshore Drive, then in 2019, opened their own restaurant, Union Place.

With its recent updates, the interior of Union Jack's is clean, cozy, super cute, and full of fun and games. The business is two retail spaces put together with a large and spacious outdoor patio behind the building. Patrons can enjoy a variety of indoor and outdoor games such as darts, billiards, or horseshoes. Weekly events include live music, karaoke, and trivia.

Homemade food and signature recipes comprise the "pub grub" menu at Union Jack's. A variety of sandwiches includes the colossal pub club, "Unequaled in Knoxville," as the menu states. Order a grilled brat or Angus beef frank and add on another for $4.50. Try a warm pita with house hummus, "Veggie delicious!" Cheeses, dips, house-made sides, and soup of the day or Guinness chili in a bread bowl are other tasty choices.

Union Place is located just off Kingston Pike on Chambliss Avenue. When you find it, you will know, "This must be the place!" It has a large parking lot and, I must say, the most beautiful restaurant courtyard in Knoxville. Union Place features much of the same great entertainment as Union Jack's along with the same homemade food, just on a larger scale.

Left: Union Jack's English Pub on Northshore Drive
Center left: Entry at Union Jack's
Center right: Monte Cristo and hand-cut fries
Right: Patio at Union Place

Start with a melty Guinness beer cheese with pretzels or tortilla chips, poutine with brown gravy, or salt-n-vinegar cod "fries" with house-made caper tartar sauce. Their sandwiches are great, and I recommend trying the Monte Cristo or the Fat Tony, which they call "The Boss" of all Reuben sandwiches.

Union Place also features one of the signature dishes of Knoxville, Metts & Beans. Their take on it is a base of Guinness chili and cannellini beans topped with grilled mettwurst sausage.

4884 Chambliss Ave., 865-540-6904
unionplacebar.com

Order your half-pound Angus burger cooked at Union Place simply as "pink" or "no pink." Substitutions of a 10-ounce grilled chicken breast or plant-based Beyond Burger are also available.

HOLLY'S GOURMET MARKET

Neighborhood gathering place

"**I** came to have breakfast . . . just like everyone else in town," one of Holly's friendly staff and I finish the sentence together and laugh as she welcomes me into the bustling restaurant. Part of the huge success of Holly's Gourmet Market is due to the sharp, well-trained, and friendly staff, led by experienced general manager Adrienne Knight and featuring the culinary work of one of Knoxville's top chefs, Holly Hambright.

Gourmet Market was opened by Eric Nelson in the 1980s around the Homberg area. Eric's market specialized in upscale cookware and kitchen gadgets along with a foodie's dream of imported cheeses, meats, decadent chocolates, flavorful teas, and other treats. Eric took the opportunity to move his shop across the street where he also began offering sandwiches, and Gourmet Market and Cosmo's Café became a neighborhood gathering place. Eric's untimely passing following a battle with cancer in 2014 stunned and saddened the community.

In 2015, Holly Hambright returned to Gourmet Market, where she began her culinary career prior to leaving her hometown of Knoxville. After traveling and cooking around the world, Holly opened eateries in Homberg, Old North Knoxville, and the downtown, but finally settled into the newly named Holly's Gourmet Market where she offers her creative take on Southern and internationally inspired dishes.

Holly's offers all-day breakfast and lunch seven days a week until 2:30 p.m. There is something for everyone on the breakfast menu from house-made granola with Greek yogurt to biscuits and gravy and breakfast burritos. Collard greens with your breakfast? Welcome to the South!

Left: Beautiful bennie
Center: Frog in the Ditch breakfast plate
Right: Entryway and outdoor seating at Holly's

Lunch offerings include soups, quiche, salads, quesadillas, and a collection of sandwiches including a daily market special, "Crust Country" sandwich based on various regions of the country.

Catering is a major part of Holly's repertoire. With a large kitchen area, the staff can prepare for events such as corporate lunch meetings, private dinners, receptions, or weddings of up to 500 guests. They will go on site or clients can even book the spacious restaurant for private events in the evening.

The pandemic brought about family meals and meal kits that can be ordered and picked up or delivered. Visit Holly's Gourmet Market soon for a unique taste of Knoxville!

5107 Kingston Pike, 865-584-8739
gourmetsmarketandcafe.com

For the ultimate in sweet treats, visit Magpie's Bakery in Old North Knoxville opened by Holly's sister, Peggy!

ABRIDGED BEER COMPANY

Perfect pairings

"**D**id you hear about the guy who wanted to open a brewpub in his own neighborhood, and his best friend is the chef?" Well, yes, I did hear that one from the guy himself, Jesse Bowers. Jesse attended school at the University of Tennessee and graduated with a degree in plant sciences. But Jesse had developed a love of brewing beer at home, which ultimately led to his new career.

Looking near his home in the Bearden area for a spot for his brewpub, Jesse found an old 1950s garage. His best friend from elementary school in Elizabethton, Joey Trott, came on board as chef. Joey earned a degree in culinary arts from Walters State. After working in Australia, cooking at the Biltmore Estate, and working as a private chef, Joey chose to return to East Tennessee. Together, Jesse and Joey opened Abridged Beer Company in 2017.

I became aware of Abridged through a Facebook post saying we should all go try the burger at Abridged. So I thought, OK, I'll go try it. My next thought was: where is it? Searching around the neighborhood, I, too, found that 1950s garage—just off Kingston Pike on Lockett Road. This off-the-beaten-path location has not been a problem whatsoever for Abridged. In addition to social media, Jesse and Joey credit the Knoxville beer community with spreading the word about their venture. They immediately developed a loyal following.

As well as collaborating on food and beer, Jesse and Joey also formed a partnership with an unlikely ally: Erin Presbyterian Church. Through a variance with the city with the idea of opening up the neighborhood with shared parking, guests of their brewpub park in the church parking lot.

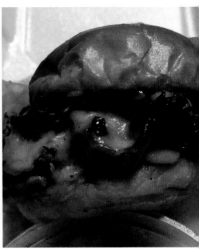

Left: Burger and side of house-made potato salad

Center: Owners Jesse Bowers and Joey Trott

Right: Best-selling Abridged burger

Jesse explains the term "Abridged" means to shorten without losing the sense. His focus in brewing began as creating "abridged" versions of craft beer—lower alcohol content but full of flavor. He has created over 300 varieties.

That famous Abridged burger—seven ounces of all-beef ground brisket, applewood-smoked bacon, caramelized red onion, fried brussels sprout petals, and house aioli on a brioche roll—accounts for 70 percent of Abridged food sales. Other offerings include a special burger of the month and an amber beer maple syrup chicken sandwich. Drop by Abridged to experience Jesse and Joey's flavorful pairings!

100 Lockett Rd., 865-200-8059
abridgedbeer.com

The original idea was for Chef Joey to have a food truck—now Abridged does! Look for your Abridged favorites all around town!

JACOB'S GRILL & DELI

Connecting with customers since 1974

Jacob Kamar grew up in Jerusalem but came to the United States in 1970. After working as a hotel receptionist in Jerusalem, he became maître d' in a restaurant in Washington, DC. Jacob visited a friend in Knoxville, loved the area, and decided to stay.

In 1974, Jacob opened his own restaurant on Middlebrook Pike. When he found the empty building on the then two-lane road, there was an old Time Out Deli sign, along with pasture to one side and an industrial area on the other. The building first began as someone's home.

While Jacob's Grill & Deli is not in the neon lights, traffic, and flashy restaurants of Kingston Pike, it has been a refuge for laborers and locals in the community to have a nourishing meal with Jacob, who works the dining room, like any great restaurant owner should. "I'm going to baby them, I'm going to spoil them," Jacob says. "I want to make a connection with my customers, they want to be recognized." I know this is true because before I talked to him, I sat and watched him speak to every guest. Jacob's motto is, "What can I do for you to make your day pleasant?" Noting that, "For me, it does matter." He has had some of his regular customers since 1980.

With a menu somewhere between a deli and a restaurant, Jacob offers something for everyone. He cares a lot about what he sells and strives to use the highest-quality ingredients. Guests can choose from a menu of salads, deli sandwiches, grilled sandwiches, gyros, and more. They even have lasagna!

When I ask about one of Jacob's signature and most popular items, Steak in a Sack, that's when things get interesting. First of all, what is it? Part Greek and part Middle Eastern, Steak in a Sack is grilled steak in a pita, with your choice of cheese, mushrooms,

Left: Popular grilled Reuben on rye

Center: Owner Jacob Kamar

Right: Steak in a Sack

tomato, lettuce, or onion. Its origin? Well, while it is an actual dish, Jacob tells me it was the name of a restaurant near where he worked in Washington, DC. "The name of the restaurant was Steak in a Sack?" I queried. Yes, the place they hung out in after work was a restaurant called—Steak in a Sack.

Visit Jacob and his wife Rhonda at their eatery Monday through Saturday until 3:30 p.m.

5307 N Middlebrook Pike, 865-584-6671
facebook.com/jacobsgrilldeli

On your way to see Jacob and Rhonda, you can drive past the historic Middlebrook house, built in 1845 by Gideon Morgan Hazen. It is one of the oldest existing frame houses in Knoxville.

AUBREY'S

Real comfort, real food, real good

"Oh, we've been there about four times already," I remember telling Randy Burleson shortly after his Aubrey's on Papermill opened in 2007. My friends and I love supporting local business owners who are doing good things around town. The longtime restaurateur has built a mutual relationship of respect with members of the community. Community stewardship is key to the Aubrey's mission, with support of education, schools, and teachers at the forefront.

Randy's hospitality lineage can be traced back to the legendary Regas restaurant family. As a student at the University of Tennessee, he became an intern at the popular Grady's Good Times, one of the Regases' most popular concepts, which grew to 52 locations.

Randy opened his first Aubrey's in 1992. The brand has now grown to 14 locations, all in East Tennessee. Many diners return for the consistency in food and service found at Aubrey's. Whether having a nice dinner with family, celebrating a birthday, or lunch with friends, Aubrey's warm, inviting space and smiling employees always make it a good destination.

Aubrey's menu is filled with fresh and comforting selections. Each locations features its own daily food and drink specials, with choices like beef tenderloin, tomato bisque, or specialty salads. Other popular items include burgers, sandwiches, steaks, seafood, and pasta.

Another of Randy's investments in the neighborhood was Bistro by the Tracks, which did start by the tracks but moved to the new Brookview Town Centre with an upscale look and refined menu. Duck confit, sea bass, house-made pasta, and bouillabaisse of smoked salmon are some of the rotating dishes.

Grilled farm-raised salmon tacos with avocado, pico de gallo, jack cheese, and chipotle cream accompanied by Parmesan spinach

Located right next door is Drink, a fun midtown lounge and wine bar featuring live jazz, hand-crafted cocktails, and a small-plate menu provided by the kitchen of Bistro by the Tracks. Three stations of wine-tasting systems contain a total of 48 ever-changing varieties available for self-serve to guests.

Enjoy exploring the many local restaurants of Burleson Brands all around Knoxville and the East Tennessee area!

6005 Brookvale Ln., 865-588-1111
aubreysrestaurants.com

Aubrey's commitment to communities includes serving the highest level of fresh and locally sourced meats, fish, vegetables, and fruits possible.

HAM'N GOODYS

Don't forget the lemon cookies

"Do you want a Ham'n Goodys cookie?" a local service owner asked me. Having just had some moist, flavorful Ham'n Goodys cookies a few days prior, I replied, "Yes!" thinking, what a perfect, locally made treat to keep on hand for visitors, guests, and clients.

Ham'n Goodys was opened in a small house on Northshore Drive in 1978 by three brothers-in-law, Jim Brakebill, Ray Hicks, Leroy Shoemaker, and Leroy's wife, Emily. Their idea was to help folks with prepared food for an old-fashioned, East Tennessee dinner. Carry-out became a dining trend in the 1980s for busy people in Knoxville. At Ham'n Goodys, their honey-baked hams, sugar-cured and honey-basted, became their most requested item, as pork has always been the most popular meat in this area. Customers could also order hors d'oeuvres trays for parties or picnic lunches, and, of course, pastries.

A best-selling sweet at Ham'n Goodys was always the tea cake, still popular today. Passed down from a family recipe, the sugar cookie has a cake-like consistency, offering a delightful surprise when bitten into. These days, the lemon cookie, created by Leroy, has taken over in popularity. Although asked throughout the years, the Shoemakers never gave out any of their beloved family recipes.

Over time, Leroy and Emily moved the business across the street, and also took Ham'n Goodys to many different locations and even different cities. When they were ready to sell the long-standing business, they looked to one of their food vendors, Dale Harold. Dale bought the business in 2016, then added a Cedar Bluff location at Middlebrook Pike in 2019 and a shop downtown on Gay Street in 2020.

Left: Hot ham and provolone cheese with mango chutney, pasta salad
Center: Dining room at the Northshore location
Right: Ham'n Goodys on Northshore Drive

Today, Dale continues to provide sweet treats to towns all around East Tennessee while building the brand with the Ham'n Goodys cookie truck. Look for the truck in Dandridge, Newport, Morristown, Greeneville, Johnson City, Bristol, and Kingsport, as well as Maryville and Chattanooga, among others. Check the monthly schedule to experience Ham'n Goodys in your town.

Catered box lunches and cookie trays as well as holiday boxed dinners are popular choices from Ham'n Goodys. Pick up or enjoy local delivery or have baked goods shipped to family and friends anywhere in the lower 48.

314 Northshore Dr., 865-584-2246
hamngoodys.com

Check out Ham'n Goodys fundraising options to raise money for your organization, sports team, or school group!

ALADDIN'S CAFÉ

Where everything is done with magic

In one of the most famous folktales of the 1001 Arabian Nights, Aladdin's genie could grant him wishes. In real life, a big blue genie can lead you to Al Albanna's new location for his American-Mediterranean delights at Aladdin's Café on Kingston Pike.

Al came to America from Palestine and lived in New Jersey until he visited a friend in Knoxville. He then decided he wanted to stay in this beautiful place that was safe and where the people were nice and friendly. For six or seven years, he worked at a Time Out Deli on Central. Eventually, he bought the place and ran it for 15 years. Finally, Al decided to move his deli to the other side of town in February 2020. His regular guests didn't mind the travel as long as they could find Al, and everything was going well until the shutdown for the pandemic one month later.

Because of his new location, the pandemic has been especially hard on Al. Because his was considered a new business, the café was ineligible for the PPP loan, so he used up his savings to keep Aladdin's going. It was difficult to find employees, food costs soared—a bottle of oil went from $18 to $43—and certain items such as to-go plasticware, cups, and bags were hard to find. He felt like he was going to battle every day.

One day, Al's neighbor from his old Central location, Jeff Miller, owner of J&L Car Lot, came in for lunch and found Al running the entire restaurant by himself. The following day, Jeff showed up and volunteered to help out, and he has worked all day every day since. That's the kind of loyalty and determination you find in East Tennessee.

Al serves up food made with high-quality ingredients that cause guests to notice the difference. "Anything in a pita," is on

Top left: Entrance to Aladdin's Café on Kingston Pike

Top right: The "Al"-talian

Bottom left: Look for the big blue genie at Aladdin's Cafe

Bottom right: Owner Al Albanna

the best-seller list. Gyros, shawarma, and falafel are healthier items that are grilled, with almost everything made from scratch including the falafel, tahini, and tzatziki sauces. Al even does steak-in-a-sac in the old Ali Baba Deli style. Try a Greek salad, a specialty sub such as the "Al"-talian (best toasted), or an Aladdin's burger—fresh pattied beef, gyro meat, feta, and tzatziki sauce. You know you want to stick around for homemade desserts—Al's famous baklava, and daily varieties of pies, cakes, and cookies.

Visit Al Monday through Saturday from 11 a.m. 'til 8 p.m. and find some magic at Aladdin's Café.

7025 Kingston Pike, 865-312-9581
aladdincafetn.com

When I comment that the dining room at Aladdin's is spotlessly clean, Al tells me many of the city health inspectors eat here.

STIR FRY CAFÉ

Old City comes to West Knoxville

Do you ever find yourself shopping and running errands in West Knoxville, wishing you could be having your next meal in an eclectic, locally owned eatery like you might find downtown? That restaurant exists! In 1993, 10 years before the redevelopment of Market Square, restaurateur Kenny Siao created Stir Fry Café in the Gallery shopping center. His vision was a place reminiscent of Knoxville's Old City, which realized a renaissance after the 1982 World's Fair, featuring patio seating, live jazz, and an art gallery atmosphere, but with plenty of that West Knoxville parking.

Entering Stir Fry Café naturally transports you back in time with the black-and-white checkerboard floor and neon sign to the phones and lavatory. You might notice Billy Idol, Soft Cell, or other '80s hitmakers playing through the speakers. Patrons can enjoy or purchase paintings and art directly off the walls. You feel a sense of calm of a less stressful time gone by.

After moving to Knoxville from Malaysia, Kenny had a dream to bring the food of his homeland of Southeast Asia to the community. He realized his goal by focusing on sushi, Asian, and Thai cuisine; the concept was successful from the beginning. Kenny also opened other restaurants in Knoxville before his untimely passing at the young age of 43. His family kept the restaurants going until selling each of them to local investors.

Whether craving a comforting plate of rice and veggies or a hot and spicy soup, diners can choose from a vast menu at Stir Fry Café. Traditional starters include Thai spring rolls, steamed or seared dumplings, or crab rangoons. Add a healthy seaweed salad or tom yum or tom kha soups. Many cooked, raw, or vegan

Left: Dining room of Stir Fry Café

Center top: Thai spring roll with house duck sauce and spicy mustard

Center bottom: Chef's special: Stir Fry Combo

Right: Stir fry your way from the vast menu

sushi rolls are available with select half-price rolls for Monday, Wednesday, and Saturday dine-in.

Rice and noodles offers a choice of a create your own bowl or house recipes, including curry basil rice, Singapore noodles, and bo pho—shrimp, beef, chicken, and basil in beef broth. A bento box presents a sampling of everything. In a stir fry your way plate, add whatever you want for a protein. It's all up to you at Stir Fry Café!

7240 Kingston Pike, Ste. 128, 865-588-2064
stirfrycafeknoxville.com

Search through the restaurant for the two photos of Kenny Siao still looking over Stir Fry Café!

SULLIVAN'S FINE FOOD

A Rocky Hill neighborhood favorite

Rocky Hill is a neighborhood full of everything one might need: schools, churches of various denominations, a local independently owned small grocery store, medical offices, a hardware store, fitness centers, a wellness studio, plenty of housing, its own Christmas parade, and a great family-friendly restaurant— Sullivan's Fine Food.

"They want to order a salad and eat out on the patio under that big shade tree," I mused. Longtime general manager Jonathan Roberts agrees. That big tree is a sugar maple that owner Charles Irvine built a patio for his restaurant around. Charles began his restaurant career at Copper Cellar, then helped operate Patrick Sullivan's downtown for years before finally moving out to the Rocky Hill area in West Knoxville to open his own Sullivan's in 1994. Unlike the saloon feel of the downtown Patrick Sullivan's, Charles's new Sullivan's was focused on fine food in a family-oriented environment. He created a menu with an emphasis on good food, fresh ingredients, the best meats, and great service.

The best-selling item at Sullivan's is the Northshore salad— grilled chicken, feta cheese, candied pecans, and craisins with a balsamic vinaigrette. Lunch diners also have choices between dishes like pot roast and catfish with sides like fried corn or sweet potato casserole.

Appetizers at Sullivan's include a pimento cheese dip with bacon jam and onion rings served in a martini glass. For dinner try a dish inspired by one of Charles's trips to Alaska: fresh grilled salmon with an orange sriracha glaze, served with pineapple and jasmine rice.

Sullivan's in the Rocky Hill neighborhood

One fallout from the pandemic was having to temporarily suspend Sunday brunch. General manager Jonathan explains that brunch is a harder service to execute with a need for more experienced staff during a nationwide employee shortage. He is very thankful for the Rocky Hill community, which supported Sullivan's with a strong to-go business before and during the pandemic.

7545 S Northshore Dr., 865-694-9696
sullivansfinefood.com

Planning a party or special event? Sullivan's also has a private dining space that can accommodate up to 35 guests.

CHEZ GUEVARA

Hidden in plain sight

Located in an unsuspecting suburban plaza (called Suburban Plaza) is a true hidden gem of Knoxville—Chez Guevara Restaurante Mexicano. Somewhat of a speakeasy for foodies, the popular destination has no sign to lead the way, but if you know, you go. Someone might tell you, someone might take you, but owner Kevin Diffley states that, "Most everyone who comes, comes back."

In business for 40 years, Kevin does no advertising. In this tight-knit community, he has had some of the same employees for 35 years and new hires must be recommended by current employees. Kevin presides over the dining room, seating guests on a first-come, first-served basis and letting them know that they will do their best for them. You get in when you get in. And you are happy about it. I can't recall when I've seen so many happy people packed into one small space.

Kevin studied economics and Spanish literature in college, hence the Mexican restaurant. Beginning under the name La Paz, Kevin's partners wanted to take the corporate route for their venture. Kevin decided to let them have the name and go their own way while he continued keeping it local. He emphatically notes that he wouldn't have done anything different.

The new name is fitting, derived from the rebel and revolutionary, whose mere picture symbolizes counterculture. Che Guevara grew up as a chess player and an avid reader. His upper-class childhood home contained more than 3,000 books.

The eclectic decor and artwork of Chez Guevara is collected from everywhere. Despite their best-selling dish being the Elvis burrito—chicken, black beans, guacamole, sour cream, and queso—

Left: Eclectic decor in the dining room

Center left: Tasty Tex-Mex meal

Center right: Friendly service of Chez Guevara

Right: Fresh tortilla chips with two kinds of salsa with every meal

and multiple images of Elvis everywhere you look, Kevin insists that it is merely Tennessee kitsch and that people bring Elvis pictures and art to him. Other best sellers include the spinach con queso and black and blue nachos.

Try a quesadilla stuffed with Alaskan king crab, salmon with cream cheese and cucumber salsa, pork tenderloin, or chorizo. Or maybe go for a chile relleno with spinach and jack cheese fried in blue corn meal or one filled with raisins, almonds, and mole sauce.

So search out this revolutionary eatery, and tell them Paula sent you.

8025 Kingston Pike #A, 865-690-5250
facebook.com/chez.guevara.knoxville

Kevin Diffley has never owned an Elvis record. Maybe swing by with one for him.

FINN'S RESTAURANT & TAVERN

Authentic Irish

Finn's Restaurant & Tavern is named after Finn McCool. In Irish mythology, Finn is a hunter and warrior, claimed to be of extraordinary height, somewhat of a giant. This giant story goes along very well with all the big stories of the location of Finn's, the Baker Peters House, as well known as a restaurant site as it is to be haunted.

Most folks who have worked inside the historic antebellum home have stories of unexplained happenings to tell. The home was built in 1930 and occupied by Dr. James Harvey Baker, who, it was rumored, had been treating Confederate soldiers during the Civil War. After confronted by Union soldiers, Dr. Baker claimed no support of either side of the war, but that he treated anyone who needed medical attention. Dr. Baker was shot and killed by Union soldiers that day, and Abner, who later also died a tragic death, is said to haunt the old dwelling.

In 2019, Jon Ferrie, who had previously owned another Irish restaurant in town, the Irish Times, along with Dan Hale, brought something new and beautiful to the Baker Peters House. Nestle into one of the small dining rooms for an intimate dinner and conversation, surrounded by dark wood furniture and rich green accents. Finn's also has plenty of space for tavern-style dining along with live music nightly. Although most of the restaurant is located on the second floor, the Abner Room on the first floor is wheelchair accessible and available to reserve for private dining.

Finn's menu features traditional Irish dishes and some with a twist. Guests can enjoy starters of Irish spring rolls filled with corned beef and cabbage, steamed blue mussels, tavern nachos with corned beef and Swiss, and Scotch eggs with strawberry serrano jam. Try a

Left: Full Irish breakfast
Center: Beautiful seating area in dining room
Right: Fish and chips

seasonal hummus or hot pimento cheese dip. Entrees include salmon leap and chicken curry among others. End with a decadent bread pudding or Guinness chocolate mousse.

Sunday brunch is offered 11 a.m. until 2 p.m., when you can experience an Irish breakfast plate with tenderloin, eggs, applewood bacon, home fries, grilled tomato, and, of course, beans. Check ahead for Finn's daily food and drink specials!

9000 Kingston Pike, 865-357-0894
finnstavern.com

Finn's occasionally offers a ghost tour of the Baker Peters House, which is an after-hours guided investigation led by Knoxville's local mediums. Investigate Finn's soon!

TOKEN GAME TAVERN

Geeks, drinks, food, and fun

The Windsor Square shopping center in West Knoxville has become a destination for visitors to partake in any number of quirky activities—shop for wigs at King's Beauty, find a treasure at Amvets Thrift Store, get lost in Burlington Coat Factory, catch a two-dollar movie at AMC Classic Theater, marvel over a pay phone on the sidewalk, or . . . enter another world altogether.

"Yes, it's a local business; they also own Token Game Tavern," a friendly employee told me. I had been gushing over my fantastic burger topped with roasted brussels and Havarti at the home of '80s and '90s pop culture and modern burgers, Bit Burger. The blank expression on my face probably gave it away that I wasn't familiar with Token Game Tavern. The next time I visited Windsor Square, I went a few doors down and peeked in. "Oh. Oh . . . this is a whole thing!" I thought to myself, and I was immediately in.

Courtney and Chris Barry are the masterminds behind the brand, which opened in 2017. The space is filled with games—arcade games and board games, as well as video game consoles. Servers are dressed in costume, and Courtney and Chris regularly host special events and cosplay parties so guests can also join the fun. On the menu, inventive tacos, nachos, and flatbreads join variations of slider dogs, cozy grilled cheeses, pizza bites, and old-school Kraft mac & cheese with chili. Enjoy a handcrafted popping soda, slushie, or vanilla iced coffee, or the innovative drinks from the Galactic Cantina or Alchemist's Workshop. Breakfast cereal shots are available all day.

Bit Burger came next, bravely opening in 2021 despite the ongoing pandemic. Much smaller than Token Game Tavern, Bit Burger is filled with nostalgic posters, toys, and action figures

Top left: Interior of Token Game Tavern

Center left: Grown-up grilled cheese with chips and tomato bisque

Center right: Entrance to Token Game Tavern

Right: Vanilla cream soda

Bottom: Multitude of games available in dining room

and focuses on fresh and local craft burgers with handmade accompaniments that can be delivered to Token. They are also known for over-the-top shakes and desserts.

The pièce de résistance of Courtney and Chris's trilogy is the new Space Bar. "I love, love, love it!" I told Courtney. "It's so smart!" Guests are greeted by aliens or space travelers and guided into the small, dark, and intimate "Ark" spaceship to the experience. Menus light up when opened. A mocktail menu was presented when alcoholic beverages were passed over. Food and drink are delivered by flashlight and time given to guests to take pictures or videos.

213 N Seven Oaks Dr., 865-770-3870
tokengametavern.com

Space Bar is an experience like no other! Enjoy the out-of-this-world food and drink menu!

SAMI'S CAFÉ

A family tradition

"Are you gonna post it?" Bassam Natour asks after noticing me photographing my plate on one of his many daily trips into the dining room at Sami's Café. Bassam is one of the Natour brothers, who each operate their own eateries in Knoxville. Older brother Pete runs his namesake Pete's in the downtown area, Basel has Rami's Café in Old North, and Bassam owns Sami's Café, named after his father, in the Franklin Square shopping center on the west side of town.

After emigrating from Palestine, Bassam's father worked as a cook in a restaurant in Washington, DC. In 1973, the family moved to Knoxville. Here, Bassam's father and his uncles owned and operated the popular Copper Kettle and Helma's restaurants where Bassam and his brothers helped out and learned the restaurant business.

All three brothers earned college degrees, and Bassam worked as a manager for UPS before operating his own café in the Medical Arts Building downtown from 1993 until suffering a heart attack in 2008. After recuperating, he helped at Pete's until the landlord of Franklin Square, Bill Hodges, recruited him to open a café in the shopping center in 2009. Bill's foresight paid off when Sami's Café brought many new customers to the square. Saturday breakfasts were packed with guests lined up down the sidewalk. With the need for more space, Bill expanded the dining room for Sami's.

The Natour brothers believe in family first—all offering breakfast and lunch service to have evenings free for family time. Part of their success comes from focusing on one location and being there from open to close. Bassam knows that by taking care of customers and providing good quality food at a good value, and plenty of

Left: Meat and two lunch: turkey and dressing, mashed potatoes, okra, and roll
Center: Owner Bassam Natour
Right: Lunch special: beef stew, fried okra, macaroni, and cornbread muffin

it, a business will do well. Bassam loves to talk and communicate with his customers and build relationships with them. He is also considerate of his employees; I watched him say goodbye to each of them by name at the end of their shift.

Sami's offers breakfast specials, combos, and other homemade fare such as daily meat and three lunch specials created with recipes from Bassam's father. Bassam also credits his father's knowledge and expertise for the brothers' success, even through the pandemic, as he taught them to save for the future. Bassam states they owe everything to their father, Sami. Stop by and see what it is all about at Sami's Café!

9700 Kingston Pike, Ste. 5, 865-531-7900
samiscafe.com

Show up at Sami's Café for lunch on Thursday when you can try one of Knoxville's specialty dishes, Metts & Beans: mettwurst served with white beans.

TENNESSEE TAP HOUSE

Showcasing the best of East Tennessee

Many culinary careers began at Knoxville's Regas Restaurant. Patti Anderson began her culinary career and her life with husband Don at the legendary establishment. For 20 years, Don Anderson was employed with Regas Restaurant, working his way up to general manager and eventually president in 1991, under owner Bill Regas. Don was later a managing partner at Italian Market Grill, Tennessee Grill, and Baker Peters. In 2005, he became owner of New Knox Brewery, then opened Mulligan's in 2006. In 2017, he opened Tennessee Tap House with Patti and their daughter, Macy.

Don, Patti, and Macy dedicated Tennessee Tap House to showcasing local flavors as well as celebrating traditions of East Tennessee—good food, music, sports, and, especially, University of Tennessee football. In keeping with current trends and noticing the expanding local beer market, the Andersons decided to place a focus on beer and feature a rotating selection of 36 taps.

Patti and her family went through a devastating blow in 2021 when Don unexpectedly passed away at age 65. Patti had a desire to continue the restaurant and, although much of her background was working in marketing and the mortgage business, she had also learned the restaurant business while working with Don. She enjoys the work, keeping busy and interacting with people, and now alternates days in the restaurant with Macy.

Patti has acclimated well to being a female business owner, even building clear partitions between booths with son Matt during the pandemic. Her loyal locals supported the restaurant so strongly during that time that Patti realized more fully the importance of supporting local business.

Left: Creative dish served on classic pewter plate

Center: Owner Patti Anderson

Right: Beautifully landscaped exterior of Tennessee Tap House

Though beer is a big draw, guests also come into Tennessee Tap House particularly for the food. Everything is made to order from scratch, based on recipes the family created as they opened. Sauces, dressings, seasonings, and even Boursin cheese is made in house. Grass-fed beef is provided from local Double L Farms, owned by longtime friends of the Andersons all the way back to when their kids went to school together.

Best sellers at Tennessee Tap House include pizza, burgers, and fish and chips. Have a plate to honor General Robert Neyland with Neyland nachos (house-made potato chips, salsa, black beans, and Schulz Brau Beer queso) or try Sister Sarah's sampler (chicken tenders, pretzel bites, and potato skins).

Guests can enjoy brunch every Sunday, and Wednesdays through Saturdays feature live music.

350 N Peters Rd., 865-394-9425

tennesseetaphouse.com

Patti's key to success in the restaurant business: "You've gotta have it in your blood."

K TOWN TAVERN

Gathering place with a great history

Knoxville's K Town Tavern, descended from one of the oldest restaurants in Tennessee, the Peerless, has its roots in Tennessee football. The Peerless story began in 1938 when John Kalogeros, a hot dog street vendor in Johnson City, opened a restaurant specializing in barbecue. On New Year's Day 1940, guests gathered in to watch Tennessee play in the Rose Bowl. For the special occasion, John treated patrons with Grecian salads and steaks. After hearing folks comment that his steaks were the best steaks they had ever tasted, John immediately changed the focus of the restaurant, and the rest is steakhouse history.

John Kalogeros's son Jim took over the business in 1947, and it is now run by John's grandson, Gary. Gary and wife, Nia, expanded and opened a Peerless in Knoxville in the building that formerly housed the second Grady's Good Times restaurant. Noticing the trend of fine dining was being replaced by more casual dining with emphasis on supporting local communities, Nia and Gary adapted the Knoxville Peerless concept to celebrate the city, even highlighting one of its nicknames.

The "Don't Throw Down on K-Town" campaign was premiered on billboards around the city by the Keep Knoxville Beautiful organization in 2004. K Town Tavern honors Knoxville with their handcrafted fare, artisan reclaimed wood tables, 40 varieties of craft beer on tap, and 101 crafted bourbon and whiskey selections, including small-batch bottles. K Town Tavern is perfect for sports enthusiasts with its 20 premier HDTVs or for those who want to enjoy the outdoors on the spacious indoor/outdoor patio.

You can still experience their famous Kalogeros Grecian salad—mixed greens, tomato, cucumber, pepperoncini, kalamata olive,

Left: Brick oven Greek pizza

Center: Exciting Tennessee-themed entryway to dining room

Right: Lounge area and bar

celery, peas, creamy feta, and a Grecian vinaigrette. Another Greek favorite passed down from the Peerless is the Big Fat Greek Opa flaming cheese appetizer, fired tableside, with grilled pita bread.

Entrees include fajitas, pulled pork, blackened mahi, shrimp scampi, and tavern baked mac & cheese. Enjoy a carne asada steak sandwich, barbecue bacon & cheddar chicken, or a burger topped with classic toppings or pimento cheese, mac & cheese, or bleu cheese. Wood-fired pizzas are assembled and baked in guest view in the lobby.

320 N Peters Rd., 865-691-8144
ktowntavern.com

Keeping up with the current trends, K Town Tavern is partnering with a craft axe throwing business in its former banquet area. Stop by for some fun!

CALHOUN'S

The taste of Tennessee

After restaurateur Mike Chase's success with his Copper Cellar restaurants, he turned to barbecue for his next endeavor and in 1983, opened the first Calhoun's in a two-story barnlike building, complete with a silo, which paid tribute to the farming heritage of East Tennessee. Soon after, the team participated in the National Rib Cook-Off and won! Calhoun's hickory-smoked baby back ribs earned the title of Best Ribs in America.

Calhoun's has grown to nine locations in East Tennessee. The Bearden Hill location was a microbrewery before the nationwide microbrewing trend took off. The Tennessee River location is connected to Volunteer Landing, a mile walkway along the river, and features an outdoor dining patio and private dining room upstairs, overlooking the river. It is also accessible by boat.

Another popular concept in the Copper Foods family for beach-loving mountaineers is Chesapeake's, providing fresh seafood flown in daily. The first Chesapeake's has been a mainstay of the downtown area since 1983. A second location opened in 2018 on Parkside Drive in a beautifully revamped 26,000-square-foot warehouse. The new location can easily seat 350 guests and an additional 200 in their special event center.

Copper Foods Smoky Mountain Brewery, which opened in 1996 in Gatlinburg, is the oldest craft brewery in East Tennessee. In the '90s, local microbrewed beer was not popular. How times have changed! When the craft beer movement exploded, they were ready for it and opened the Turkey Creek location in 2008 focusing on in-house brewed beer, hand-tossed pizza, wings, burgers, steaks, and Italian specialties.

Left: Rustic interior of Calhoun's
Center: Original Calhoun's location on Kingston Pike
Right: Calhoun's Trio: baby back ribs, chicken tenders, and hickory-smoked pork

"Have you eaten at Corner 16 yet? It's so good!" many locals say on my tours. What is Corner 16? The newest Cooper Foods concept! Where is Corner 16? Bob Kirby Road, just off Middlebrook Pike, near the Ball Camp community. "Meet me at the corner" is the idea—meet family or friends for lunch, after work for a drink, for dinner and to watch a game, to enjoy live entertainment or for outdoor dining around a cozy firepit. Southern comfort food is the focus. Think deviled eggs, and the best seller, smothered chicken—hand-breaded fried chicken with a country garden gravy. Old-fashioned cream and house-made phosphate sodas are a unique addition.

Enjoy eating your way through the Copper Foods family of restaurants!

10020 Kingston Pike, 865-673-3444
calhouns.com

Smoky brisket burnt ends wrapped in bacon served with Tennessee whiskey barbecue sauce is a Calhoun's best seller!

PORTON MEXICAN KITCHEN

New to the neighborhood

Some people choose wine by the picture on the label. Do I choose restaurants to eat at by stylish signage? Well . . . yes, I sometimes do. I was drawn into Porton Mexican Kitchen by the bright pink sign with the old west motif. I remember thinking, "That place has got to be good." And it is.

"Do you have a chef?" I ask owner Victor Montes as I peer back into the kitchen. He gives me a look. "You cook too? You do everything here?" At this point Victor has already welcomed and seated me, taken my order, made me the most delicious tortilla soup with pulled chicken and chunks of avocado along with some grilled chicken fajitas, served my lunch, and come back to check on me, along with everyone else in the restaurant, and is now rolling silverware with his daughter, Atziry, who comes in sometimes to help him out. Victor and his wife even designed the layout and look of the restaurant, and his sister-in-law contributed the colorful Día de los Muertos paintings.

Having worked in restaurants since coming to the states in 1998, Victor took in many different styles of cuisine and cooking. To create his menu, he draws from his experiences and puts his own spin on traditional and new dishes. He intentionally keeps the menu relatively small, and emphasizes that everything is made from scratch.

Start with some freshly made crispy tortilla chips and salsa with a hint of sweetness. In addition to tacos, burritos, enchiladas, quesadillas, or fajitas, guests can also choose from more unique dishes such as milanesa (breaded and deep-fried chicken breast) or tilapia Veracruz (tender grilled fish with poblanos, a tomato-based sauce, and olives).

154

Left: Pasta al mojo de ajo

Center: Owner Victor Montes with daughter Atziry

Right: Tilapia Veracruz

Being in a new shopping center in a growing area, Porton faced some challenges after opening in 2019. Business picked up during the pandemic due to Porton's to-go orders. People in the neighborhood became familiar with the restaurant through delivery services. Victor began to notice some new customers ordering three times a week.

Victor noted that "everything in life comes with challenges." His new restaurant has been one of his biggest challenges but also a big success. Visit soon for a delicious meal and excellent service!

9623 Countryside Center Ln., 865-247-4914
portonmexicankitchen.net

Don't miss the Mexican street corn with queso anejo, mayo, chile, and lime. Yes, they will cut it off the cob for you.

NICK & J'S CAFÉ

Worth the drive

Knoxville loves a burger. I've eaten a lot of great burgers in
Knoxville. But when the Nick & J's Brownstone burger
was placed in front of me, a half pound of fresh ground beef,
hand-pattied that morning, towering with bacon and cheddar,
grilled onions, and onion straws, dripping with barbecue sauce,
and skewered by a steak knife, it was the first time I ever felt
intimidated by a burger.

Najwan Natour descends from a restaurant family. After
emigrating from Palestine in the 1960s, Najwan's father and uncles
owned Helma's and the Copper Kettle restaurants. After learning
the business working with his father, Najwan operated the Time
Out Deli and Froggy's before opening Nick & J's Café, named for
his sons, Nicholas and Jordan, in 2009. Najwan's father and mother
now come into his restaurant to help out along with his wife, Linda.

At Nick & J's, everything is made fresh daily using locally
sourced meats and market produce. If you go there for breakfast,
consider some Tennessee-based Clifty Farms Country Ham with
buttermilk pancakes or an omelet with Swaggerty's sausage from
the other side of town in Kodak.

For lunch, try a soup or a featured salad such as the Kronos
Greek or sandwich specialties like the chicken cordon bleu. But
the burgers, oh the burgers! The Habibi Delight is an eight-ounce

Nick & J's Café has been featured on *CNN Headline News*, Fox
News *Breakfast with Fox & Friends*, Food Network's *Top Places to
Eat*, and *USA Today*.

Left: Nationally recognized burgers
Center: Dining room of Nick & J's
Right: Brownstone burger with house-made chips

burger topped with half a pound of pastrami, swiss, onion straws, a fried egg, and spicy mustard. Or give me that Whammy—a half-pound cheeseburger in between two grilled cheese sandwiches. Meat and vegetable specials are offered daily, homemade from family recipes.

The most common compliment I read about Nick & J's is that it is "worth the drive!" After being closed for eight weeks during the pandemic, their loyal community base really stepped up with take-out orders and large tips for employees to share in order to keep a favorite diner going. Nick & J's, they know food!

1526 Lovell Rd., 865-766-5453
knoxvillerestaurantstn.com

CAZZY'S CORNER GRILL

Artistic dining with a healthy touch

At the intersection of Northshore Drive and Pellissippi Parkway in West Knoxville is the Northshore Town Center. With walkable shopping, a school, office workspace, dining, residences, and green space, this master-planned community mimics an old-fashioned downtown living plan and neighborhood but with an upscale modern design, amenities, and conveniences. Townhomes, condos, apartments, and single-family houses offer views of the Tennessee River and the Great Smoky Mountains. Residents and visitors might have a workout, get a haircut or manicure, pick up groceries, or have a great meal out at Cazzy's Corner Grill, all in the town center.

Cazzy's Corner Grill was opened in 2012 by Jim Cornett. With 20 years experience in the restaurant business, he previously worked with Copper Cellar, Cappuccino's, Fleming's Prime Steakhouse, Cozy Mel's, and Macaroni Grill. Cornett was an opening partner with P. F. Chang's, helped open Dead End BBQ, and opened and operated Wok Hay Fresh Asian Diner before selling it to Ruby Tuesday. He created Cazzy's to be a neighborhood corner grill for families.

Cazzy's was also eventually sold, and in 2017, the new owners, along with then chef Kyle Russell, took home *Cityview* magazine's top chefs competition first-place award for both the categories of entree (lavender seared yellowfin tuna with fire-roasted brussels, edamame aioli, and hemp seed) and dessert (Reeve honey pistachio and pomegranate panna cotta with bee pollen and milk crumbles). That winning panna cotta is still on the menu along with current chef Annie Fletcher's 2021 first-place dessert—dark chocolate ganache cake with rum caramel sauce.

Left: Stylish dining room
Center left: Grilled Carolina trout, quinoa, slaw, herb potato salad
Center right: Cazzy's Corner Grill on Northshore Drive
Right: Dark chocolate ganache cake with rum caramel sauce

Chef Annie has something in common with Chef Kyle—an artistic background. When I learned that all of her menu items start as sketches in her sketchbook, it made perfect sense. She creates and serves dishes at Cazzy's that are just as beautiful, colorful, and textural as they are flavorful and delicious.

Starters feature dishes like hummus and seafood gumbo, while entrees range from vegetarian curry and grilled trout to bison burgers and cajun pork chops.

Sunday brunch offers an andouille sausage or garden veggie omelet, egg or crab cake Benedicts, huevos rancheros, Southwest potato hash, chicken and waffles, and blueberry Belgian waffles.

2099 Thunderhead Rd., 865-694-6311
cazzys.com

Cazzy's also partners to create healthy dishes recommended by the Temple of Human Performance, which educates clients on a holistic way to wellness and a healthier lifestyle.

LAKESIDE TAVERN

Waterfront dining

Waterfront dining: the dream we all dream. Take a drive to West Knoxville for a beautiful waterfront dining setting at Lakeside Tavern at Concord Park. The tavern concept was developed by the legendary Regas restaurant family who opened Riverside Tavern near downtown Knoxville. They then sold the tavern concept to restaurateur Bob McManus with an agreement to build six additional places. The Lakeside Tavern building was patterned after the original Riverside Tavern as were the Westside Tavern on Kingston Pike and Parkside Tavern on North Peters Road.

Lakeside Tavern overlooks the community of Concord, which began to develop in the 1850s and is now listed on the National Register of Historic Places as Concord Village Historic District. Concord became a major part of the Tennessee marble production and shipping industry beginning in the 1880s. Although most of the remnants of Concord's marble production are now gone, a foundation of a crusher used to make terrazzo chips is still visible in Concord Park. Today, visitors flock to Concord Park for all types of outdoor sports and recreation, for boat rental at the marina, on lost marble hunts, and for a relaxing lunch or dinner at Lakeside Tavern.

Start with appetizers like avocado lime shrimp or fried asparagus or try one of their delicious salads. For your main, you can order specialties like grilled ahi tuna, filet mignon, or a brick oven pizza.

Lakeside Tavern's Sunset Room can accommodate up to 55 guests for private dining and parties for lunch or dinner.

Left: The Sunset dining room

Center: Pistachio Parmesan Carolina mountain trout

Right: Beautiful views of Concord Marina

The tavern also has decadent desserts like crème brûlée cheesecake and a Kahlua fudge brownie.

The Parkside Tavern McManus created on North Peters Road was renamed Parkside Grill. At Parkside Grill you'll start with warm, salted-top bread, served with every meal. Go for the grilled Atlantic salmon with mustard dill sauce or Southern delights such as potato cracklins with beer cheese and bacon or pork chops infused with a Wild Turkey marinade.

Lakeside Tavern and Parkside Grill are now both part of Diverse Concepts Ltd., which has branched out of Knoxville and also includes Liberty Park Grill in Clarksville at the Marina, Harrison's in Clinton, and Bullfish Grill, Blue Moose, Mellow Mushroom, Johnny Carino's, and Timberwood Grill, all in Pigeon Forge.

10911 Concord Park Dr., 865-671-2980
lakeside-tavern.com

CONNORS STEAK & SEAFOOD

Committed to a superior dining experience

Through the past several decades, restaurateur Mike Connor has helped create and carry on the fine dining scene in Knoxville. After beginning his career with Steak & Ale in 1973 and working with the company in different states, in 1982 he was recruited from Dallas back to Knoxville by Bill, Grady, Gus, and Frank Regas to help open their first Grady's Goodtimes. He brought along college friends Rick Federico and Kevin Thompson and eventually the popular Grady's concept grew to 52 locations.

In 1992, Mike set out with colleagues Kevin Thompson, Tony Watson, Brian Keyes, and Bo Connor to open his new restaurant, the Chop House in the Shops at Franklin Square. The Chop House has grown to a regional collection of nine locations—in Tennessee—West Knoxville, North Knoxville, Kodak, Sevierville, Murfreesboro, Hendersonville, and Kingsport, along with Augusta, Georgia, and Dayton, Ohio. By 2004, Connors Steak & Seafood opened in the Turkey Creek shopping center in Knoxville, followed by Huntsville, Alabama, in 2008; Fort Myers, Florida, in 2012; Franklin, Tennessee, in 2016; and Sarasota, Florida, in 2017.

Keeping with the values passed down through the Regas ranks led to much success. Connor Concepts places emphasis on providing a good value, consistency, quality, and friendly customer service, with an intensive training program for team members. The scene is set with warm colors and rich woods in their restaurants for a comfortable, relaxing meal with soft jazz in the background.

The Chop House offers lunch from 11 a.m. until 4 p.m. with entrees specially priced at $12, $13, and $14. Dinner includes

Left: Elegant dining room

Right: Fish & chips with dill caper sauce

USDA Choice steaks grilled over 1,800 degrees along with add-ons such as béarnaise sauce, bleu cheese butter, cold water lobster tail, or the chef's daily preparation. Other guest favorites are 12-hour slow-roasted prime rib, French cut pork chops, and rosemary grilled chicken. Soups, salad dressings, sauces, and desserts are made in house using fresh ingredients.

Connors Steak & Seafood also features a specially priced lunch menu and dinner of seasoned prime cuts of aged beef and fresh seafood grilled over mesquite wood. Indulge in a gourmet salad, lobster crab bisque, or the Isle of Shellfish (Blue Point oysters, jumbo crab meat, jumbo shrimp, lobster tail, and king crab leg).

10915 Turkey Dr., 865-966-0933
connorsrestaurant.com

Mike Connor was awarded Tennessee Restaurateur of the Year and has been inducted into the East Tennessee Business Hall of Fame. Connors Steak & Seafood is listed in the Best 100 Steakhouses by *Forbes*, Best Steakhouse in All 50 States by *Business Insider*, and is consistently ranked as the #1 restaurant in Knoxville on Tripadvisor.

SEASONS INNOVATIVE BAR & GRILLE

Classical cuisine in a new American bistro

"We had a fantastic meal at Seasons 101 in Sevierville," one of the guests from my tour told me. Then, in typical Southern-style direction giving, "It's right there, downtown, you know, on the corner, at that new hotel." I knew exactly where he was talking about. One of Knoxville's top chefs, Deron Little, has opened an extension of his Seasons restaurant in Sevierville at the Historic Central Hotel. Favorite restaurants are always a topic of discussion and usually include Chef Deron's Seasons Innovative Bar & Grille. "Oh, and I love Seasons at Turkey Creek!"

Once while having a late lunch at Seasons, a table full of chefs sat near me. It was an outing arranged by one of them to try various menu creations and dissect techniques used by Chef Deron. Deron Little is recognized as a Certified Executive Chef by the American Culinary Federation of which he has been a member for over 20 years. His early career found him working for major corporations such as Stouffers, as well as Omni, Wyndham, and Marriott Hotels. Later he opened his first restaurant, Tahoe South, in downtown Greenville, South Carolina.

In 1996, Chef Deron was recruited to Knoxville as executive chef for Gettysvue Country Club. When that property was sold, he moved to Fox Den Country Club, where he developed a loyal following for his dishes created with an artistic flair and remained there until 2006. He then went on to open his Seasons restaurant in West Knoxville. In 2013, he relocated the restaurant to the Turkey Creek shopping complex.

Left: Scallop special
Center left: Seasons at Turkey Creek
Center right: Side house salad
Right: Seasons' dessert tray

At Seasons Innovative Bar & Grille, Chef Deron is dedicated to high-quality food preparation and presentation. He uses classical cooking techniques to create seasonal menus focused on fresh ingredients. Your meal will begin with focaccia bread, pesto hummus, and butter for the table. Choose starters from options like wild-caught shrimp and prosciutto brussels sprouts. Follow your appetizer with a salt-roasted beet salad or seasonal soup.

Entrees at Seasons include gourmet sandwiches and burgers or larger dishes like a rack of lamb.

Saturday and Sunday brunch is available from 11 a.m. until 2 p.m.

11605 Parkside Dr., 865-392-1121
seasons-cafe.com

Be sure and let your server bring Seasons' dessert tray by your table to select a sweet ending to a fabulous meal!

DADDY MAC'S DOWN HOME DIVE

Who's your daddy?

They say some people work their whole lives to get back home. It seems restaurateur Dave McFarland has worked a long time to now be able to bring a bit of his home, his grandparents, to us. Many people I talk with tell me their grandmother taught them to cook. One of my most prized possessions is a notebook of recipes handwritten by my grandmother and passed down to me. Dave pays a tribute to all four of his grandparents with his new restaurant—Daddy Mac's Down Home Dive.

The original Daddy Mac was Dave's paternal grandfather who was known as a man of his word and instilled a strong work ethic in others. Mama Mac taught Dave about unconditional love and the importance of faith. Dave's maternal Nana shared her wisdom and emphasized having a good time. But it was Dave's Papa who was the great cook and who introduced him to the world of flavor.

Dave's new concept lies at the very far end of Turkey Creek in the building where he ran a Wild Wings Café for 14 years. Dave went from Wild Wings franchises to two of his own Daddy Mac's, one in Asheville and the impressive Knoxville site with its large pond and fountain in front of the rustic-style building. After planning the idea since 2016, the time was finally right and Daddy Mac's opened in 2021, in spite of the pandemic.

The restaurant is steeped in family tradition and pickle juice, but don't call it merely a barbecue restaurant. Neither is Daddy Mac's a traditional Southern restaurant. Think elevated pub fare with a creative Southern flair where everything is made from scratch including smoked meats. The stars of the show are the

Left: Daddy Mac's Down Home Dive at Campbell Lakes Drive
Right: Pulled pork sandwich, Daddy's mac & cheese, smoked potato salad, brew-b-q beans

Bar-B-Cue-Terie boards. They're adorable and a great way for guests to try many popular items such as brisket and pulled pork or their famous pickles.

Guests can also build a salad bar in a jar with a base of lettuce and their choice of protein and toppings, delivered to the table in a mason jar with house-made dressing. Shake well, pour onto a plate, and enjoy!

11335 Campbell Lakes Dr., 865-288-0088
eatatdaddymacs.com

Daddy Mac's provides two large dining rooms plus a bar along with a stage for live music offered throughout the week. Check their website for their schedule and daily food and drink specials!

APPLE CAKE TEA ROOM

It's all about tradition

While Pigeon Forge and Gatlinburg might welcome travelers with a myriad of log cabin pancake houses, Knoxville welcomes guests with a log cabin tearoom. Mary Henry opened the Apple Cake Tea Room in 1983 with a good friend with similar interests. Their plan was to open a gift shop, but on an exploratory trip to the gift buyers' market, they made a stop at a then popular tearoom, Miss Daisy's in Nashville. It was then that they decided to create their own tearoom in Knoxville.

At the time, the area they chose for their new venture in West Knoxville was mostly farmland and open fields. Soon, they moved to a log cabin structure that was built across the street, which fit the tearoom style perfectly. After three years in business, Mary's friend moved away, and she continued the business in the same style, with her motto, "It's all about tradition." Mary's mother and grandmother taught her how to cook, and the tearoom decor is composed of their family antiques. A private room that seats 35 is available upstairs and frequently used for parties. The tearoom has welcomed five generations of families for birthday parties, bridal and baby showers, and the popular little girl tea parties.

The tearoom takes its name from the first recipe Mary perfected for her menu—apple cake. After developing the remainder of the menu, Mary has kept it basically the same through the years. Mini bran muffins with butter begin every meal. The most popular dish is the tea room medley—chicken salad, chips, banana nut bread with cream cheese filling, and glazed fruit. Other unique choices are the pineapple boat filled with chicken salad, or heartier dishes such as roast beef with gravy or a stuffed potato. The cornucopia dessert is a rolled French pizzelle cookie filled with ice cream and sautéed

Top left: Cake and tea
Top center: Tea room medley
Top right: Upstairs dining room
Bottom: Cornucopia dessert

bananas and topped with a choice of caramel or chocolate sauce. The house recipe drink is friendship tea, a sweetened spiced tea.

Mary's daughter and other family help her at the tearoom, and it has also been a great first job for many young people. In addition to a loyal local clientele, which kept the tearoom open during the pandemic with takeout orders, the Apple Cake Tea Room hosts guests from all across the country every Monday through Saturday, 11 a.m. to 2:30 p.m.

11312 Station W Dr., Ste. A, 865-966-7848
facebook.com/apple-cake-tea-room

Apple Cake Tea Room has been featured in national travel and specialty magazines and books such as *Touring America, Interstate Gourmet, Blue Ridge Country, Taste of Home, Women's Day*, and *Southern Lady*.

RESTAURANTS A-Z

A Dopo, 46
516 Williams St.

Abridged Beer Company, 126
100 Lockett Rd.

Aladdin's Café, 134
7025 Kingston Pike

Ale'Rae's Gastro Pub and
Coffee Bar, 76
937 N Broadway

Alice's Diner, 80
4405 N Broadway

Apple Cake Tea Room, 168
11312 Station W Dr., Ste. A

Aubrey's, 130
6005 Brookvale Ln.

Balter Beerworks, 44
100 Broadway SW

Barley's Taproom & Pizzeria, 62
200 E Jackson Ave.

Bistro at the Bijou, 2
807 S Gay St.

Boyd's Jig & Reel, 60
101 S Central St.

Broadway Market, 4
900 E Hill Ave., #130

Burger Boys, 94
2400 Chapman Hwy.

Calhoun's, 152
10020 Kingston Pike

Cazzy's Corner Grill, 158
2099 Thunderhead Rd.

Central Filling Station, 66
900 N Central St.

Chez Guevara, 140
8025 Kingston Pike, #A

Connors Steak & Seafood, 162
10905 Turkey Dr.

Copper Cellar, 106
1807 Cumberland Ave.

Cruze Farm Ice Cream, 16
445 S Gay St., Ste. 103

Daddy Mac's Down Home
Dive, 166
11335 Campbell Lakes Dr.

Downtown Deli, 8
800 S Gay St.

Emilia Italian, 40
16 Market Square

Fai Thai Kitchen, 12
522 S Gay St.

Farmacy, 120
5018 Kingston Pike

Fin-Two Japanese Ale House,
56
122 S Central St.

Finn's Restaurant & Tavern,
142
9000 Kingston Pike

Good Golly Tamale, 58
112 S Central St.

Gosh Ethiopian, 116
3609 Sutherland Ave.

Gus's Good Times Deli, 102
815 Melrose Place

Ham'n Goodys, 132
314 Northshore Dr.

Hard Knox Pizzeria, 112
4437 Kingston Pike

Holly's Gourmet Market, 124
5107 Kingston Pike

Inskip Grill, 86
4877 N Broadway, Ste. 5

J. C. Holdway, 30
501 Union Ave.

Jacob's Grill & Deli, 128
5307 N Middlebrook Pike

K Town Tavern, 150
320 N Peters Rd.

Kaizen, 50
127 S Central St.

KoPita, 10
524 S Gay St.

Lakeside Tavern, 160
10911 Concord Park Dr.

Landing House, 100
1147 Sevier Ave.

Litton's Market, Restaurant
& Bakery, 88
2803 Essary Rd.

Long's Drugstore & Fountain,
118
4604 Kingston Pike

Maple Hall, 20
414 S Gay St.

Matt Robbs Biscuits & Brew, 6
800 Market St.

Nama Sushi Bar, 14
506 S Gay St.

Nick & J's Café, 156
1526 Lovell Rd.

Not Watson's Kitchen + Bar, 26
15 Market Square

OliBea, 48
211 S Central St.

Oliver Royale, 28
5 Market Square

Original Freezo, 70
1305 N Central St.

Paysan Bread & Bagels, 54
804 Tyson St.

Pete's, 32
540 Union Ave.

Phoenix Pharmacy and
Fountain, 18
418 S Gay St.

Pizzeria Nora, 72
2400 N Central St.

Plaid Apron, 110
1210 Kenesaw Ave.

Porton Mexican Kitchen, 154
9623 Countryside Center Ln.

Preservation Pub, 42
28 Market Square

Rami's Café, 78
3553 N Broadway

Red Onion, 114
3625 Sutherland Ave.

Saloon 16, 104
1706 Cumberland Ave.

Sam & Andy's, 84
2613 W Adair Dr.

Sami's Café, 146
9700 Kingston Pike, Ste.5

Schulzes Schnitzel Kitchen, 64
126 Bernard Ave.

**Seasons Innovative Bar
& Grille, 164**
11605 Parkside Dr.

Smilin' Jack's Café, 92
4620 Mill Branch Ln.

SoKno Taco Cantina, 98
3701 Sevierville Pike

Southern Grit, 52
126 S Central St.

Steamboat Sandwiches, 74
2423 N Central St.

Stir Fry Café, 136
7240 Kingston Pike, Ste. 128

Stock & Barrel, 24
35 Market Square

Sullivan's Fine Food, 138
7545 Northshore Dr.

Sunspot, 108
2200 Cumberland Ave.

**Suttree's High Gravity Tavern,
22**
409 S Gay St.

Tennessee Tap House, 148
350 N Peters Rd.

The Amber Restaurant, 90
6715 Maynardville Pike

The French Market Creperie, 36
412 Clinch Ave.

The Oak Room by Abridged, 68
109 W Anderson Ave.

**The Original Louis' Restaurant,
82**
4661 Old Broadway

The Tomato Head, 38
12 Market Square

Token Game Tavern, 144
213 N Seven Oaks Dr.

Union Place Bar & Grill, 122
4884 Chambliss Ave.

Yassin's Falafel House, 34
706 Walnut St.

Ye Olde Steak House, 96
6838 Chapman Hwy.

APPENDIX

BEARDEN

Abridged Beer Company, 126
Farmacy, 120
Gosh Ethiopian, 116
Hard Knox Pizzeria, 112
Holly's Gourmet Market, 124
Long's Drugstore & Fountain, 118
Plaid Apron, 110
Red Onion, 114
Union Place Bar & Grill, 122

CAMPUS/CUMBERLAND

Copper Cellar, 106
Gus's Good Times Deli, 102
Saloon 16, 104
Sunspot, 108

CEDAR BLUFF

Calhoun's, 152
Finn's Restaurant & Tavern, 142
K Town Tavern, 150
Sami's Café, 146
Tennessee Tap House, 148
Token Game Tavern, 144

DOWNTOWN

A Dopo, 46
Balter Beerworks, 44
Bistro at the Bijou, 2
Broadway Market, 4
Cruze Farm Ice Cream, 16
Downtown Deli, 8
Emilia Italian, 40

Fai Thai Kitchen, 12
The French Market Creperie, 36
J. C. Holdway, 30
KoPita, 10
Maple Hall, 20
Matt Robbs Biscuits & Brew, 6
Nama Sushi Bar, 14
Not Watson's Kitchen + Bar, 26
Oliver Royale, 28
Pete's, 32
Phoenix Pharmacy and Fountain, 18
Preservation Pub, 42
Stock & Barrel, 24
Suttree's High Gravity Tavern, 22
The Tomato Head, 38
Yassin's Falafel House, 34

FARRAGUT

Apple Cake Tea Room, 168
Cazzy's Corner Grill, 158
Connors Steak & Seafood, 162
Daddy Mac's Down Home Dive, 166
Lakeside Tavern, 160
Nick & J's Café, 156
Porton Mexican Kitchen, 154
Seasons Innovative Bar & Grille, 164

FOUNTAIN CITY

Inskip Grill, 86
Litton's Market, Restaurant & Bakery, 88
Sam & Andy's, 84

HALLS

The Amber Restaurant, 90
Smilin' Jack's Café, 92

OLD CITY

Barley's Taproom & Pizzeria, 62
Boyd's Jig & Reel, 60
Fin-Two Japanese Ale House, 56
Good Golly Tamale, 58
Kaizen, 50
OliBea, 48
Southern Grit, 52

OLD NORTH

Ale'Rae's Gastro Pub
and Coffee Bar, 76
Alice's Diner, 80
Central Filling Station, 66
Paysan Bread & Bagels, 54
The Oak Room by Abridged, 68
Original Freezo, 70

The Original Louis' Restaurant, 82
Pizzeria Nora, 72
Rami's Café, 78
Schulzes Schnitzel Kitchen, 64
Steamboat Sandwiches, 74

SOUTH/SOKNO

Burger Boys, 94
Landing House, 100
SoKno Taco Cantina, 98
Ye Olde Steak House, 96

WEST HILLS

Aladdin's Café, 134
Aubrey's, 130
Chez Guevara, 140
Ham'n Goodys, 132
Jacob's Grill & Deli, 128
Stir Fry Café, 136
Sullivan's Fine Food, 138